open**doors**

REPORT ON INTERNATIONAL EDUCATIONAL EXCHANGE

Hey-Kyung Koh Chin

Institute of International Education

D1316632

Contents

Overview: International Students in the U.S.: *The Big Picture* 2

Financial Contributions 4   *Their Origins* 8   *U.S. Destinations* 10   *Colleges and Universities* 12

Fields of Study and Student Profile 14   U.S. Students Abroad 16   Intensive English Programs in the U.S. 20

International Scholars in the U.S. 22   Global Competition 24   **Data Tables**: International Students 25

Study Abroad 57   Intensive English Programs 69   International Scholars 79   Methodology 87   Acknowledgments 96

OPEN DOORS is a long-standing, comprehensive information resource on over 565,000 international students in the United States in 2004/05 and on over 191,000 U.S. students who studied abroad for academic credit in 2003/04. The Institute of International Education, the largest and most experienced U.S. higher education exchange agency, has conducted an annual statistical survey of the internationally mobile student population in the United States since 1948, with U.S. government support since 1972.

Suggested Citation: *Open Doors 2005: Report on International Educational Exchange*, 2005. Hey-Kyung Koh Chin, ed. New York: Institute of International Education.

565,039 international students were studying in the U.S. in 2004/05, a decline of 1.3% from the previous year.

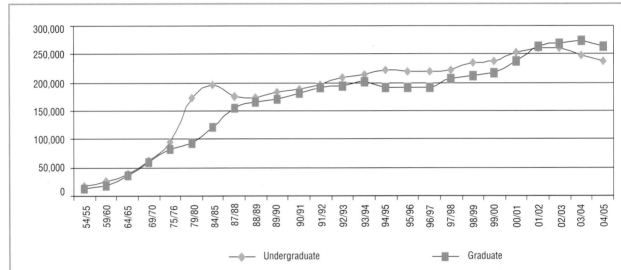

Undergraduate   Graduate

Graduate international students continued to outnumber undergraduate international students in 2004/05, a trend that began in 2001/02.

Academic Level	Int'l Students	Total U.S. Students*	% of U.S. Enrollment
Associate's	65,667	4,592,854	1.4
Bachelor's	173,545	7,386,905	2.3
Graduate**	264,410	2,015,110	13.1
Other***	61,417	-	-
Total	**565,039**	**13,994,869**	**4.0**

Graduate international students were 13% of all U.S. graduate enrollments.

* College Board Annual Survey of Colleges data on U.S. higher education enrollment

** Includes first professional degrees

*** Primarily includes international students participating in Optional Practical Training and Intensive English Programs

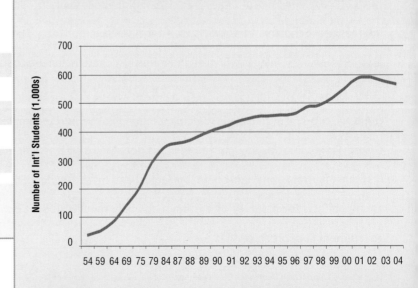

After several years of strong growth, international student enrollments have declined over the past two years.

Year	Int'l Students	Annual % Change	Total Enrollment	% Int'l
1954/55	34,232	-	2,499,800	1.4
1959/60	48,486	2.6	3,402,300	1.4
1964/65	82,045	9.7	5,320,000	1.5
1969/70	134,959	11.2	7,978,400	1.7
1974/75	154,580	2.3	10,321,500	1.5
1979/80	286,343	8.5	11,707,000	2.4
1984/85	342,113	0.9	12,467,700	2.7
1985/86	343,777	0.5	12,387,700	2.8
1986/87	349,609	1.7	12,410,500	2.8
1987/88	356,187	1.9	12,808,487	2.8
1988/89	366,354	2.9	13,322,576	2.7
1989/90	386,851	5.6	13,824,592	2.8
1990/91	407,529	5.3	13,975,408	2.9
1991/92	419,585	3.0	14,360,965	2.9
1992/93	438,618	4.5	14,422,975	3.0
1993/94	449,749	2.5	14,473,106	3.1
1994/95	452,635	0.6	14,554,016	3.1
1995/96	453,787	0.3	14,419,252	3.1
1996/97	457,984	0.9	14,286,478	3.1
1997/98	481,280	5.1	13,294,221 *	3.6
1998/99	490,933	2.0	13,391,401	3.6
1999/00	514,723	4.8	13,584,998	3.8
2000/01	547,867	6.4	14,046,659	3.9
2001/02	582,996	6.4	13,511,149	4.3
2002/03	586,323	0.6	12,853,627	4.6
2003/04	572,509	-2.4	13,383,553	4.3
2004/05	565,039	-1.3	13,994,869 **	4.0

International students were only 4% of U.S. higher education enrollments in 2004/05, although their numbers have grown dramatically since the 1950s.

* In 1997, the College Board changed its data collection process.

** College Board Annual Survey of Colleges data on U.S. higher education enrollment

THE BIG PICTURE

Throughout the history of the *Open Doors* International Student Census, there have been periods of strong growth followed by plateaus, affected by both global and domestic political and economic events. For the second consecutive year, international student enrollment in U.S. higher education showed a decline, with a 1.3% drop in 2004/05, following a 2.4% drop in 2003/04. These declines followed a year of minimal growth, and two prior consecutive years of strong growth.

The past two years of decline have been attributed to a number of factors, including a tightening of visa application review processes since September 11, 2001; perceptions and concerns abroad whether the U.S. would continue to welcome international students and whether visas could still be obtained; rising costs of U.S. higher education; strong competition from other host countries, especially the U.K. and Australia; and increased higher education capacity in several leading sending countries, such as India, China, and Korea. In 2004/05, undergraduate enrollments declined more steeply than graduate enrollments, widening the gap between these two categories of international students, a trend which began in 2001/02.

International students
$13 billion to the

State	Int'l Students 2004/05	Tuition & Fees[1] 2004/05	Living Exp. & Dependents[2] 2004/05	Less U.S. Support[3] 2004/05	Total Contribution 2004/05	State	Int'l Students 2004/05	Tuition & Fees[1] 2004/05	Living Exp. & Dependents[2] 2004/05	Less U.S. Support[3] 2004/05	Total Contribution 2004/0
Alabama	6,359	$62,825,487	$84,563,679	$46,563,140	$100,826,026	Montana	966	$12,633,046	$13,835,890	$4,613,316	$21,855,62
Alaska	439	$4,558,588	$6,647,326	$1,959,517	$9,246,397	Nebraska	3,915	$40,567,209	$57,788,993	$27,030,490	$71,325,7
Arizona	10,011	$111,147,298	$139,463,872	$71,585,645	$179,025,524	Nevada	2,846	$21,593,625	$56,358,771	$14,118,035	$63,834,3
Arkansas	2,784	$29,202,926	$38,728,195	$19,100,396	$48,830,725	New Hampshire	2,061	$47,413,612	$41,750,123	$19,006,889	$70,156,8
California	75,032	$1,168,385,432	$1,535,250,182	$699,296,050	$2,004,339,564	New Jersey	12,571	$230,026,658	$261,580,246	$132,802,758	$358,804,1
Colorado	5,496	$95,995,765	$92,195,653	$59,446,298	$128,745,120	New Mexico	2,151	$23,487,061	$32,839,771	$21,597,909	$34,728,9
Connecticut	7,138	$149,844,558	$134,431,964	$47,224,473	$237,052,049	New York	61,944	$1,127,603,203	$1,249,778,286	$683,213,647	$1,694,167,8
Delaware	2,317	$31,864,353	$32,632,785	$9,167,829	$55,329,309	North Carolina	9,029	$155,670,658	$151,627,185	$108,243,772	$199,054,0
D.C.	7,763	$171,647,432	$178,552,005	$129,678,375	$220,521,062	North Dakota	1,641	$16,468,404	$21,678,374	$7,362,095	$30,784,68
Florida	26,264	$426,977,194	$418,135,075	$219,220,851	$625,891,418	Ohio	17,952	$311,477,063	$331,632,400	$237,993,281	$405,116,1
Georgia	12,111	$182,850,154	$190,648,250	$120,298,710	$253,199,694	Oklahoma	8,454	$83,017,934	$123,235,534	$55,270,896	$150,982,5
Guam	63	$441,870	$559,067	$104,885	$896,053	Oregon	5,490	$86,806,885	$93,488,224	$44,147,252	$136,147,8
Hawaii	5,485	$47,488,896	$93,277,280	$34,176,552	$106,589,624	Pennsylvania	22,773	$499,077,579	$434,949,191	$323,269,928	$610,756,8
Idaho	1,923	$18,088,024	$29,625,546	$12,550,707	$35,162,863	Puerto Rico	976	$3,571,835	$16,102,749	$5,545,040	$14,129,5
Illinois	25,021	$461,672,317	$496,612,171	$340,916,202	$617,368,286	Rhode Island	3,043	$68,533,598	$60,682,634	$36,296,177	$92,920,0
Indiana	13,149	$231,568,212	$235,290,475	$164,711,417	$302,147,270	South Carolina	3,559	$48,236,120	$60,377,131	$41,626,013	$66,987,2
Iowa	7,675	$118,219,906	$128,226,740	$91,151,577	$155,295,069	South Dakota	665	$5,315,955	$7,565,772	$2,632,859	$10,248,8
Kansas	6,217	$62,418,346	$88,770,280	$42,657,770	$108,530,856	Tennessee	5,767	$87,217,579	$87,519,106	$56,805,442	$117,931,2
Kentucky	4,792	$54,117,570	$55,403,918	$34,220,406	$75,301,082	Texas	47,367	$493,269,190	$703,950,366	$340,471,603	$856,747,9
Louisiana	6,744	$85,518,211	$90,722,133	$41,093,928	$135,146,416	Utah	5,918	$43,247,053	$89,454,044	$40,782,698	$91,918,3
Maine	1,530	$27,181,935	$22,944,115	$15,438,435	$34,687,615	Vermont	864	$21,892,618	$14,235,890	$7,950,103	$28,178,4
Maryland	13,439	$217,087,023	$229,627,766	$154,132,527	$292,582,262	Virgin Islands	104	$1,138,176	$1,397,670	$310,104	$2,225,7
Massachusetts	27,985	$677,572,766	$628,134,462	$437,294,915	$868,412,313	Virginia	12,501	$182,768,099	$188,724,085	$103,761,500	$267,730,6
Michigan	20,879	$330,641,045	$324,726,207	$228,328,308	$427,038,943	Washington	10,674	$133,608,664	$169,838,890	$73,287,376	$230,160,1
Minnesota	8,491	$121,161,118	$134,014,938	$83,118,310	$172,057,746	West Virginia	2,567	$29,988,806	$38,964,182	$23,809,922	$45,143,0
Mississippi	2,266	$20,322,289	$31,810,466	$19,808,741	$32,324,014	Wisconsin	7,798	$156,406,216	$108,289,807	$101,987,494	$162,708,5
Missouri	9,540	$153,069,046	$158,347,591	$90,924,613	$220,492,025	Wyoming	530	$4,210,848	$8,456,707	$4,634,825	$8,032,7
						TOTALS	**565,039**	**$8,997,115,456**	**$10,025,444,159**	**$5,732,742,001**	**$13,289,817,6**

International students in the U.S. made a considerable contribution to the economy through tuition payments and cost of living expenditures.

1. 2004/05 tuition, living, and miscellaneous expenses from the College Board. These expenses are computed separately for undergraduate and graduate students and the sum of the two groups is reported here.
2. See p. 55 for *Open Doors* estimate of the percent of international students who are married. The number of spouses in the U.S. is estimated to be 85% of the number of married students. The number of children is estimated to be six for every ten couples in the U.S. The presence of a spouse increases living expenses by 25%. The presence of a child increases living expenses by 20%.
3. U.S. funding support level is computed based on the institution's Carnegie Type.

Analysis prepared for NAFSA: Association of International Educators by Jason Baumgartner and Lynn Schoch of Indiana University at Bloomington, using enrollment data from the Open Doors 2004/05 International Student Census.

contributed over
U.S. economy.

FINANCIAL CONTRIBUTIONS

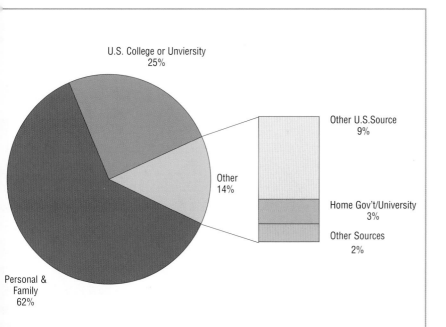

Nearly two-thirds of international students relied on personal and family funds for their U.S. studies.

Primary Source of Funds	2004/05 % of Total	% Under-graduate	% Graduate	% Other
Personal & Family	61.8	80.9	44.0	54.7
U.S. College or University	24.5	9.4	43.6	8.4
Home Government/University	2.7	2.4	2.9	2.6
U.S. Government	0.6	0.5	0.7	0.3
U.S. Private Sponsor	4.8	4.6	5.5	3.1
Foreign Private Sponsor	1.2	1.4	1.1	0.6
International Organization	0.3	0.2	0.3	0.3
Current Employment	3.7	0.3	1.3	29.6
Other Sources	0.4	0.2	0.6	0.4
Total	**565,039**	**239,212**	**264,410**	**61,417**

While 81% of undergraduate international students relied on personal and family funds for their U.S. education, only 44% of graduate international students relied on personal and family funds.

International students' presence in U.S. higher education is felt not only in the classroom and on campus, but by the impact they have on local and state economies. In 2004/05, international students contributed over $13 billion to the U.S. economy. These contributions came in the form of living expenses, including expenses for any accompanying dependents, and expenditures on tuition, fees, books, and other educational costs incurred throughout the duration of their studies.

International students funded their U.S. education using a variety of sources in 2004/05. Their primary source of funds was personal and family funds. Nearly two-thirds (61.8%) of all international students relied on personal and family funds. This was especially the case for undergraduate international students, of whom the overwhelming majority (80.9%) used personal and family funds for their studies. Among graduate international students, approximately the same percentage of students relied on personal and family funds (44.0%) as on U.S. college or university funds (43.6%). Graduate international students at large doctoral/research institutions often receive institutional funding through research grants and teaching assistantships, which primarily derive from federal or foundation grants to the host institution. Other sources of funding, including employers, U.S. and foreign governments, and international organizations, comprised a very small percentage of international students' primary source of funds.

Personal & family funds nearly two-thirds

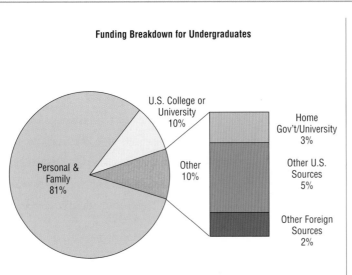

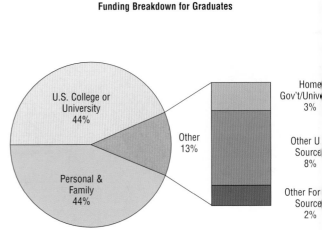

Funding Breakdown for Undergraduates

Personal & Family 81%

U.S. College or University 10%

Other 10%

Home Gov't/University 3%

Other U.S. Sources 5%

Other Foreign Sources 2%

Funding Breakdown for Graduates

U.S. College or University 44%

Personal & Family 44%

Other 13%

Home Gov't/Univ 3%

Other U Source 8%

Other For Source 2%

Undergraduate international students relied mainly upon personal and family funds, whereas graduate international students relied equally on funds from their U.S. host college or university and on personal and family funds.

Primary Source of Funds	1984/85 % of Total	1989/90 % of Total	1994/95 % of Total	1995/96 % of Total	1996/97 % of Total	1997/98 % of Total	1998/99 % of Total	1999/00 % of Total	2000/01 % of Total	2001/02 % of Total	2002/03 % of Total	2003/04 % of Total	2004/0 % o Tota
Personal & Family	66.2	63.7	68.4	67.8	67.2	67.9	67.1	67.1	66.9	67.9	65.8	67.3	61.
U.S. College or University	11.6	18.2	16.5	16.5	16.9	18.0	18.3	18.9	19.8	20.6	21.2	23.4	24.
U.S. Private Sponsor	1.9	3.1	2.2	2.1	2.3	2.3	1.9	2.7	2.5	2.7	2.5	2.2	4.
Current Employment	2.1	2.1	2.2	2.3	2.0	2.3	2.3	2.3	2.4	1.9	1.9	1.8	3.
Home Gov't/University	12.0	6.7	5.3	5.2	5.5	5.9	5.4	4.5	4.0	3.7	2.8	2.4	2.
Foreign Private Sponsor	3.0	2.2	2.5	2.9	3.5	2.5	2.8	2.7	2.4	2.0	3.3	2.1	1.
U.S. Government	2.1	2.2	1.2	1.0	0.9	0.8	0.7	0.6	0.6	0.6	0.5	0.5	0.
Other Sources	1.1	1.2	1.3	1.4	1.2	0.2	1.1	0.8	1.9	0.2	1.7	0.0	0.
International Organization	N/A	0.6	0.5	0.6	0.5	0.5	0.4	0.5	0.4	0.3	0.3	0.3	0.
Total	**100.0**	**100.0**	**100.0**	**100.0**	**100.0**	**100.0**	**100.0**	**100.0**	**100.0**	**100.0**	**100.0**	**100.0**	**100.**

Personal and family funds remained the largest source of funding for international students, followed by financial support from U.S. colleges and universities.

accounted for
of international
students' primary
source of funding.

Undergraduate Source	Doctoral/ Research Ext. & Int.	Master's I & II	Baccalaureate All	Associate's
Personal & Family	76.3	81.4	58.4	91.9
U.S. College or University	9.5	10.3	33.7	1.2
Home Gov't/University	3.9	3.0	1.4	1.1
U.S. Government	0.5	0.7	0.3	0.3
U.S. Private Sponsor	7.9	2.3	4.5	3.4
Foreign Private Sponsor	1.1	1.8	1.1	1.3
International Organization	0.3	0.1	0.3	0.2
Current Employment	0.2	0.2	0.3	0.6
Other Source	0.4	0.2	0.0	0.0

Graduate Source	Doctoral/ Research Ext. & Int.	Master's I & II	Specialized All
Personal & Family	38.1	76.1	57.4
U.S. College or University	48.6	16.2	29.7
Home Gov't/University	3.1	2.6	1.7
U.S. Government	0.8	0.4	0.5
U.S. Private Sponsor	6.1	1.8	6.6
Foreign Private Sponsor	1.0	1.3	1.2
International Organization	0.3	0.1	0.4
Current Employment	1.2	1.4	2.0
Other Source	0.7	0.3	0.6

Note: "Unknown" responses were eliminated from this analysis.

Graduate international students at Doctoral/Research Institutions had the largest percentage of U.S. higher education support, while undergraduate international students at Associate's Institutions had the highest percentage of self-financing.

FINANCIAL CONTRIBUTIONS

For the past 20 years, nearly two-thirds of international students have relied on personal and family funds to support their U.S. studies. In 2004/05, this percentage declined slightly to 61.8%, with a modest increase in the percentages of students who relied on other U.S. sources of funding. The percentage which relied primarily on funds from their U.S. college or university continued to increase slightly (24.5%), and has been ranked second for almost 20 years. A very small percentage of international students relied on other funding types as their primary source of funds.

International students' primary source of funds varied greatly by academic level and institutional type. Among undergraduate international students, those who were studying at Associate's Institutions had the highest percentage of personal and family funds (91.9%), followed by those at Master's (81.4%) and Doctoral/Research Institutions (76.3%). Students at Baccalaureate Institutions had the lowest percentage of personal and family funds (58.4%), and also had the highest percentage of host campus funds (33.7%).

In contrast, graduate international students studying at Doctoral/Research Institutions had the smallest percentage of personal and family funds (38.1%). These students tended to receive funding from their U.S. university (48.6%), usually in the form of research and teaching assistantships. Graduate international students at other types of institutions relied more on personal and family funds; students at Specialized Institutions were less likely to rely on these funds (57.4%) than students at Master's Institutions (76.1%).

India was the leading
with 80,466 students

Rank	Place of Origin	2003/04	2004/05	2004/05 % of Int'l Student Total	2004/05 % Change
	WORLD TOTAL	572,509	565,039	-	-1.3
1	India	79,736	80,466	14.2	0.9
2	China	61,765	62,523	11.1	1.2
3	Korea, Republic of	52,484	53,358	9.4	1.7
4	Japan	40,835	42,215	7.5	3.4
5	Canada	27,017	28,140	5.0	4.2
6	Taiwan	26,178	25,914	4.6	-1.0
7	Mexico	13,329	13,063	2.3	-2.0
8	Turkey	11,398	12,474	2.2	9.4
9	Germany	8,745	8,640	1.5	-1.2
10	Thailand	8,937	8,637	1.5	-3.4
11	United Kingdom	8,439	8,236	1.5	-2.4
12	Indonesia	8,880	7,760	1.4	-12.6
13	Colombia	7,533	7,334	1.3	-2.6
14	Brazil	7,799	7,244	1.3	-7.1
15	Hong Kong	7,353	7,180	1.3	-2.4
16	Kenya	7,381	6,728	1.2	-8.8
17	France	6,818	6,555	1.2	-3.9
18	Nigeria	6,140	6,335	1.1	3.2
19	Pakistan	7,325	6,296	1.1	-14.0
20	Malaysia	6,483	6,142	1.1	-5.3

The leading five places of origin represented 47.2% of international students in the U.S.

place of origin, studying in the U.S.

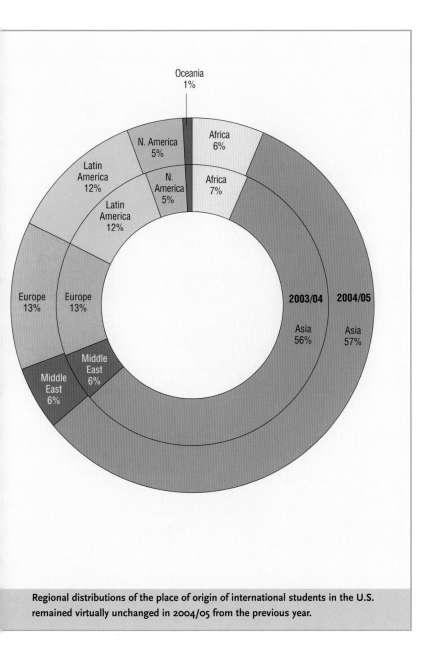

Oceania
1%

N. America
5%

Africa
6%

Latin
America
12%

N.
America
5%

Africa
7%

Latin
America
12%

Europe
13%

Europe
13%

2003/04 **2004/05**

Asia
56%

Asia
57%

Middle
East
6%

Middle
East
6%

Regional distributions of the place of origin of international students in the U.S. remained virtually unchanged in 2004/05 from the previous year.

THEIR ORIGINS

In 2004/05, 80,466 students from India were studying in U.S. higher education institutions, making India the leading place of origin of international students in the U.S. (14.2%) for the fourth consecutive year. There was a very small (0.9%) increase from the previous year, compared to double-digit percentage increases for India in two of the past four years.

China, Korea, and Japan were the next three leading places of origin, each of which showed a modest increase in enrollments from the prior year. Students from the top four Asian places of origin accounted for 42.2% of all international students in the U.S. As was the case in 2003/04, Canada surpassed Taiwan as the fifth leading place of origin, with numbers from Canada up 4.2% and those from Taiwan down 1.0%. Ten of the leading 20 places of origin for international students in the U.S. in 2004/05 were in Asia, continuing the long-standing trend of Asia being the largest sending region.

The rankings remained the same for the top eight places of origin in 2004/05. There were modest declines in the number of students from many places of origin, with the exception of double-digit declines from Indonesia and Pakistan (12.6% and 14.0%, respectively). Other fairly large declines were found in enrollments from Kenya (8.8%) and Brazil (7.1%). A large increase was found in enrollments from Turkey (9.4%), with modest increases found for Japan (3.4%), Canada (4.2%), and Nigeria (3.2%).

With respect to the global regions of origin, the distribution was practically unchanged in 2004/05 compared to the previous year.

The top 10 metropolitan
36% of all international
in the U.S.

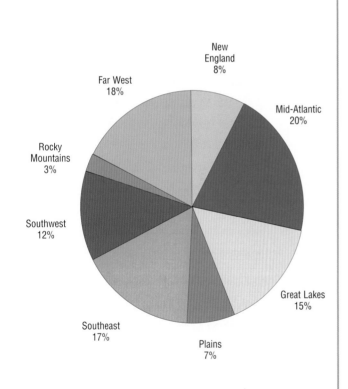

International students were studying in all regions of the U.S., with
the largest proportion in the Mid-Atlantic region.

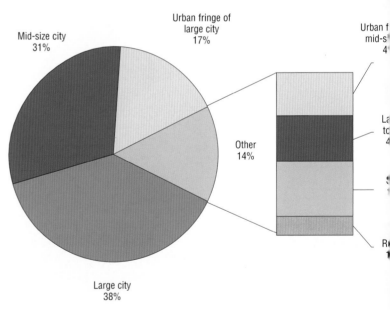

The largest proportion of international students in the U.S. was located
in large cities.

areas hosted students

Rank	Metropolitan Statistical Area	2004/05 Int'l Students
1	New York, NY	49,470
2	Los Angeles, CA	33,736
3	Boston, MA	23,336
4	Washington, DC	18,811
5	Chicago, IL	14,757
6	San Francisco, CA	13,783
7	Dallas, TX	13,611
8	Philadelphia, PA	12,707
9	Houston, TX	11,707
10	Miami, FL	11,177
	Total of Top 10	**203,095**
11	San Jose, CA	8,965
12	Atlanta, GA	8,348
13	Seattle, WA	7,503
14	Austin, TX	6,776
15	Buffalo NY	6,303
16	Phoenix, AZ	5,928
17	San Diego, CA	5,886
18	Champaign-Urbana, IL	5,858
19	Baltimore, MD	5,614
20	Ann Arbor, MI	5,608
	Total of Top 20	**269,884**

Note: Due to changes made by OMB in 2003 in the county compositions for many Metropolitan Statistical Areas, as well as the creation of Micropolitan Statistical Areas, comparisons with data prior to that in *Open Doors 2004* are not feasible.

Nearly half of all international students were studying in just 20 metropolitan areas.

International students were studying in all parts of the U.S. in 2004/05, but were highly concentrated in metropolitan areas and in certain large university towns. The vast majority of international students were studying at universities located in large and mid-sized cities (69.5%).

In 2004/05, the leading ten Metropolitan Statistical Areas (MSAs)* hosted over a third (35.9%) of all international students in the U.S. The New York City MSA hosted the most international students (49,470), followed by Los Angeles (33,736), Boston (23,336), Washington, D.C. (18,811), and Chicago (14,757). Four of the leading ten MSAs were located in the East Coast stretch from Boston to Washington, DC; two were on the West Coast; three were in the South; and one in the Midwest.

International students were also concentrated in certain geographical regions and states, varying by world region and place of origin. Many students from Asia chose to study in West Coast states such as California, Washington, and Oregon. Florida and Texas hosted larger numbers of students from Latin America, and other Spanish-speaking nations. The Northern Tier states of Michigan, Minnesota, and North Dakota attracted large numbers of students from across the border in Canada. The state which hosted the largest number of international students was California (75,032), followed by New York (61,944), Texas (47,367), Massachusetts (27,985), and Florida (26,264).

* The United States Office of Management & Budget defines these areas as a core area containing a large population nucleus, together with adjacent counties having a high degree of economic and social integration with that core.

The leading 25 institutions
18.2% of all international

Rank	Institution	City	State	Int'l Students	Total Enrollment
1	University of Southern California	Los Angeles	CA	6,846	30,000
2	University of Illinois at Urbana-Champaign	Champaign	IL	5,560	40,360
3	University of Texas at Austin	Austin	TX	5,333	50,377
4	Columbia University	New York	NY	5,278	23,775
5	New York University	New York	NY	5,140	38,188
6	Purdue University, Main Campus	West Lafayette	IN	4,921	38,653
7	University of Michigan – Ann Arbor	Ann Arbor	MI	4,632	39,031
8	Boston University	Boston	MA	4,541	29,596
9	University of California – Los Angeles	Los Angeles	CA	4,217	37,563
10	The Ohio State University, Main Campus	Columbus	OH	4,140	50,995
11	SUNY - University at Buffalo	Buffalo	NY	3,965	27,276
12	University of Wisconsin – Madison	Madison	WI	3,941	41,169
13	Texas A&M University	College Station	TX	3,721	44,813
14	University of Pennsylvania	Philadelphia	PA	3,712	23,305
15	University of Maryland College Park	College Park	MD	3,646	34,933
16	Harvard University	Cambridge	MA	3,546	19,731
17	Indiana University at Bloomington	Bloomington	IN	3,525	37,821
18	University of Florida	Gainesville	FL	3,492	48,876
19	University of Houston	Houston	TX	3,326	34,912
20	Michigan State University	East Lansing	MI	3,315	44,452
21	University of Minnesota – Twin Cities	Minneapolis	MN	3,302	50,594
22	Penn State University – University Park	University Park	PA	3,237	41,795
23	Florida International University	Miami	FL	3,155	34,876
24	Cornell University	Ithaca	NY	3,119	19,518
25	University of Arizona	Tucson	AZ	3,106	36,932

Leading 25 Host Institutions by International Student Enrollment

hosted 102,716, or students in the U.S.

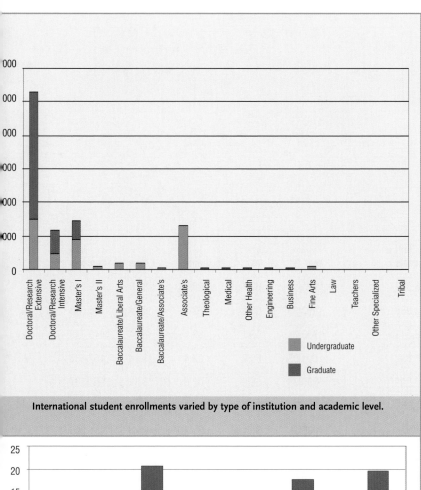

International student enrollments varied by type of institution and academic level.

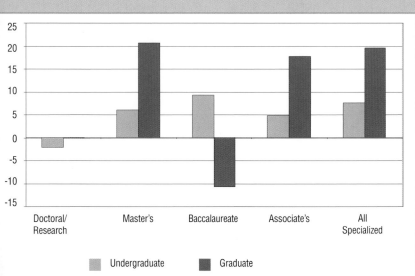

Percent changes in international student enrollment by institutional type and academic level, 2004/05.

COLLEGES AND UNIVERSITIES

Although international students studied at all types of institutions within the vast U.S. higher education system, they tended to be concentrated in a relatively small number of institutions. Of the 565,039 international students in the U.S. in 2004/05, 306,097 students, over half of the overall total, attended just 146 of the 2,042 institutions which reported enrolling international students.

The leading 25 institutions hosted 102,716, or 18.2% of all international students in the U.S. These leading 25 were all large Doctoral/ Research Institutions, each hosting more than 1,000 international students, and were based in 13 states across the U.S. Many Master's Institutions and Associate's Institutions also hosted large numbers of international students.

The 1.3% overall decline in the number of international students was not uniform across all U.S. higher education institutions, varying by institutional type and by academic level. While there was a decline in undergraduate international students at Doctoral/Research Institutions (2.1%), increases were experienced at all the other institutional types (ranging from 4.9% to 9.3%). Among graduate international students, a large decline was seen at Baccalaureate Institutions (10.7%), but increases were seen at Master's (20.7%), Specialized (19.6%), and Associate's (17.8%) Institutions. No significant change in graduate international student enrollments was reported overall in Doctoral/ Research Institutions, although individual institutions' enrollments varied widely.

The leading two fields of study,
Business & Management
and Engineering, accounted
for 193,031 or 34% of all
international students.

Year	% Male	% Single	% F Visa	Int'l Students	Year	% Male	% Single	% F Visa	Int'l Students
1977/78	75.0	77.4	78.8	235,509	1991/92	63.7	80.7	84.6	419,585
1978/79	74.1	74.7	80.7	263,938	1992/93	63.0	82.5	85.5	438,618
1979/80	72.4	78.6	82.0	286,343	1993/94	62.1	83.1	86.4	449,749
1980/81	71.7	80.1	82.9	311,882	1994/95	60.9	83.4	85.8	452,635
1981/82	71.0	79.3	84.3	326,299	1995/96	58.9	82.6	84.9	453,787
1982/83	70.9	80.1	84.0	336,985	1996/97	59.0	84.4	85.6	457,984
1983/84	70.6	80.1	83.2	338,894	1997/98	58.1	83.6	86.8	481,280
1984/85	69.8	80.4	83.5	342,113	1998/99	58.0	85.2	87.3	490,933
1985/86	70.7	80.0	81.5	343,777	1999/00	57.5	84.2	85.6	514,723
1986/87	68.9	79.7	81.0	349,609	2000/01	57.1	84.7	85.8	547,867
1987/88	67.7	79.8	79.4	356,187	2001/02	57.0	86.0	86.2	582,996
1988/89	66.5	80.9	79.0	366,354	2002/03	56.2	85.0	86.0	586,323
1989/90	66.1	80.1	78.5	386,851	2003/04	55.8	85.3	85.7	572,509
1990/91	64.0	78.5	80.6	407,529	2004/05	55.6	85.4	86.7	565,039

After almost three decades, the gender gap has narrowed; only 25% of international students were female in 1977/78, but the percentage rose to 44% in 2004/05.

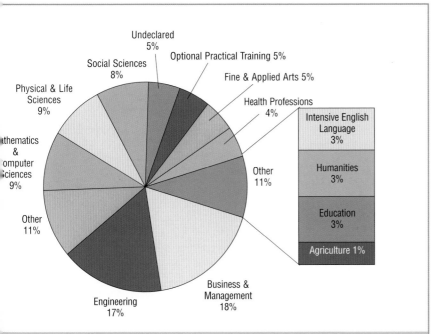

Business and management remained the leading field of study among international students, with engineering a close second.

Field of Study	2003/04 Int'l Students	2004/05 Int'l Students	2004/05 % of Total	2004/05 % Change
TOTAL	**572,509**	**565,039**	**100.0**	**-1.3**
Business & Management	108,788	100,079	17.7	-8.0
Engineering	95,220	92,952	16.5	-2.4
Other	60,273	59,700	10.6	-1.0
Mathematics & Computer Sciences	67,693	50,747	9.0	-25.0
Physical & Life Sciences	44,607	49,499	8.8	11.0
Social Sciences	54,153	46,085	8.2	-14.9
Optional Practical Training*	-	28,432	5.0	-
Fine & Applied Arts	31,882	28,063	5.0	-12.0
Undeclared	29,313	27,982	5.1	-4.5
Health Professions	25,749	26,301	4.7	2.1
Intensive English Language	15,006	16,133	2.6	7.5
Humanities	16,622	15,850	2.8	-4.6
Education	15,909	15,697	2.8	-1.3
Agriculture	7,292	7,519	1.3	3.1

* Reported within the various fields of study prior to *Open Doors 2005*

There were declines in the number of international students enrolled in most fields of study in 2004/05.

FIELDS OF STUDY & STUDENT PROFILE

Fields of Study

International students were represented across all fields of study. However, they tended to be heavily concentrated in two fields: business and management and engineering. These two fields of study accounted for approximately 193,031 international students, or 34.2% of the total in 2004/05. As in 2003/04, business and management was the leading field of study among international students, with 100,079 or 17.7% of all international students in this field. This was followed by engineering, with 92,952, or 16.5% of international students. Other leading fields included mathematics and computer sciences, physical and life sciences, and the social sciences. Double-digit increases (11.0%) were found in the physical and life sciences; on the other hand, double-digit declines were found among mathematics and computer sciences (25.0%), social sciences (14.9%), and fine and applied arts (12.0%).

Profile

The personal profile of international students has not varied much over the years. Although there have been fluctuations, the marital status of international students has remained fairly constant since the mid-1970s; in 2004/05, they were mainly single (85.4%), a larger proportion than 30 years ago. They also overwhelmingly came to study in the U.S. on an F (Student) Visa (86.7%), and again, in larger proportions now than in the mid-1970s. The one characteristic that has seen substantial change is in the gender ratio. Almost half (44.4%) of international students were female in 2004/05, whereas a quarter (25.0%) were female in 1977/78.

191,321 U.S. abroad in increase of 9.6% from the previous year.

Rank	Destination	2002/03	2003/04	2003/04 % of All Study Abroad	2003/04 % Change
	TOTAL	174,629	191,321	-	9.6
1	United Kingdom	31,706	32,237	16.8	1.7
2	Italy	18,936	21,922	11.5	15.8
3	Spain	18,865	20,080	10.5	6.4
4	France	13,080	13,718	7.2	4.9
5	Australia	10,691	11,418	6.0	6.8
6	Mexico	8,775	9,293	4.9	5.9
7	Germany	5,587	5,985	3.1	7.1
8	Ireland	4,892	5,198	2.7	6.3
9	China	2,493	4,737	2.5	90.0
10	Costa Rica	4,296	4,510	2.4	5.0
11	Japan	3,457	3,707	1.9	7.2
12	Austria	2,798	2,444	1.3	-12.7
13	New Zealand	1,917	2,369	1.2	23.6
14	Cuba	1,474	2,148	1.1	45.7
15	Chile	1,944	2,135	1.1	9.8
16	Greece	2,011	2,099	1.1	4.4
17	Czech Republic	1,997	2,089	1.1	4.6
18	South Africa	1,594	2,009	1.1	26.0
19	Russia	1,521	1,797	0.9	18.1
20	Netherlands	1,792	1,686	0.9	-5.9

U.S. students continued to study in non-traditional destinations in growing numbers; 11 of the top 20 destinations in 2003/04 were outside of Western Europe.

students studied
2003/04, an

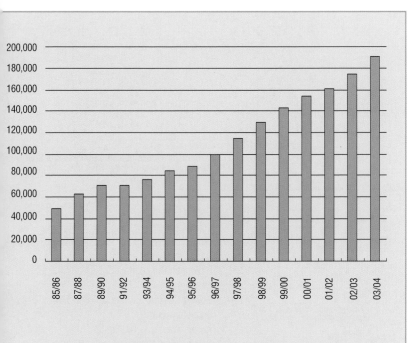

The number of U.S. students studying abroad for academic credit has increased by 47% since 1998, and by 151% in a decade.

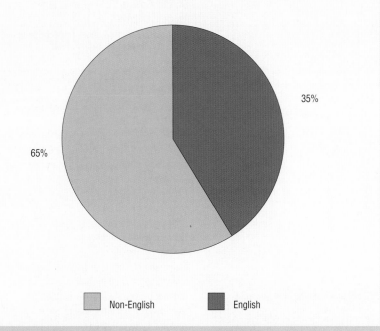

35%

65%

Non-English   English

Fifty-nine percent of students who studied abroad in the top 20 host destinations chose destinations where English is not the primary language.

U.S. STUDY ABROAD

There has been a steady increase in U.S. students' participation in study abroad for credit, a trend which continued to grow even after September 11, 2001. In 1985/86, home campuses reported just over 48,000 U.S. students who studied abroad for credit. By 2003/04, that number almost quadrupled to 191,321, rising 9.6% from the previous year. This increase follows an 8.5% increase in 2002/03, and double-digit increases in prior years. In a decade, there has been a 150.7% increase in study abroad for credit, and the total has increased 47.4% since just 1998.

The leading four destinations – United Kingdom, Italy, Spain, and France – hosted 87,957 or 46.0% of all U.S. students studying abroad in 2003/04. Australia was the fifth leading destination. Though most U.S. students studied in Western Europe, 11 of the leading 20 destinations were places in Africa, Asia, Eastern Europe, Latin America, and Oceania. Among the leading 20 destinations, 64.9% of students studied abroad in destinations where English is not the primary language.

Of the six destinations with double-digit increases in 2003/04, five were located outside of Western Europe. China had the largest increase in U.S. students abroad (90.0%), after the resumption of programs cancelled earlier due to the SARS outbreak. Other destinations with double-digit percentage increases were: Cuba (45.7%), South Africa (26.0%), New Zealand (23.6%), Russia (18.1%), and Italy (15.8%). The leading destinations which showed declines in study abroad numbers were Austria (12.7%) and Netherlands (5.9%).

Short-term study abroad accounted for 52% of all study abroad programs.

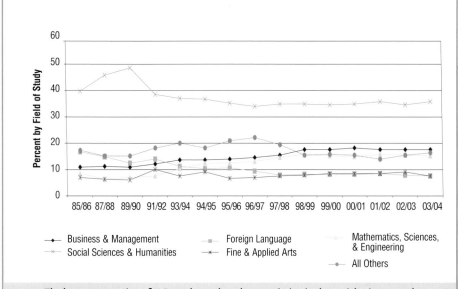

The largest proportion of U.S. students abroad was majoring in the social sciences and humanities.

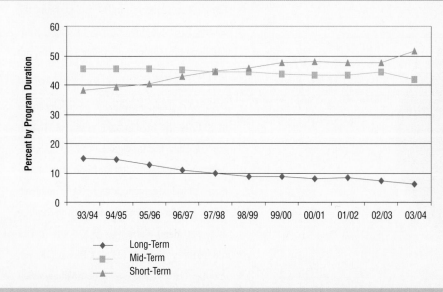

Study abroad on long-term programs continued to steadily decline in 2003/04, but short-term programs increased sharply.

Institutions with Estimated Undergraduate Study Abro Participation Rate of More Than 80%, Listed Alphabetically

Institution

Centre College
Colby College
Colgate University
DePauw University
Dickinson College
Earlham College
Eckerd College
Elon University
Illinois Wesleyan University
Kalamazoo College
Lee University
Lewis & Clark College
Lynn University
St. Olaf College
Wofford College

Institutions with More Than 1,300 Study Abroad Students, Ranked by Student Total

Institution

New York University
Michigan State University
University of California – Los Angeles
University of Texas at Austin
Penn State University – University Park
University of North Carolina at Chapel Hill
University of Minnesota – Twin Cities
University of Wisconsin – Madison
University of Georgia
University of Arizona
University of Florida
University of Pennsylvania
Boston University
University of Illinois at Urbana-Champaign
University of Washington
Indiana University at Bloomington
University of Virginia, Main Campus
Arizona State University
The Ohio State University, Main Campus
Brigham Young University

Leading U.S. Study Abroad Institutions

Percentage of Students by Program Length				
Carnegie Category	Long-Term[1]	Mid-Term[2]	Short-Term[3]	2003/04 Study Abroad Students
Research/Doctoral Ext. & Int.	6.4	41.9	51.7	114,218
Master's I & II	5.0	36.9	58.1	39,122
Baccalaureate - All	7.6	52.1	40.3	30,647
Associate's	0.2	27.0	72.8	5,776
Specialized	8.0	26.9	65.1	1,558
All Study Abroad	**6.2**	**42.1**	**51.7**	**191,321**

1 Academic or Calendar Year
2 One, Two Quarters or One Semester
3 Summer, January Term, or Fewer Than 8 Weeks

U.S. students from all institutional types preferred short-term and mid-term programs.

City	State	Undergraduate Study Abroad Students
Danville	KY	227
Waterville	ME	392
Hamilton	NY	524
Greencastle	IN	446
Carlisle	PA	419
Richmond	IN	226
St. Petersburg	FL	310
Elon College	NC	827
Bloomington	IL	433
Kalamazoo	MI	238
Cleveland	TN	725
Portland	OR	323
Boca Raton	FL	551
Northfield	MN	771
Spartanburg	SC	277

City	State	Study Abroad Students
New York	NY	2,475
East Lansing	MI	2,269
Los Angeles	CA	2,034
Austin	TX	2,011
University Park	PA	1,874
Chapel Hill	NC	1,657
Minneapolis	MN	1,644
Madison	WI	1,609
Athens	GA	1,595
Tucson	AZ	1,591
Gainesville	FL	1,537
Philadelphia	PA	1,510
Boston	MA	1,482
Champaign	IL	1,456
Seattle	WA	1,454
Bloomington	IN	1,443
Charlottesville	VA	1,427
Tempe	AZ	1,409
Columbus	OH	1,399
Provo	UT	1,335

U.S. STUDY ABROAD

Duration of Study Abroad

While mid-length programs (semester or quarter) are still popular among students who study abroad, short-term programs have steadily grown in popularity, chosen by over half (51.7%) of all study abroad participants in 2003/04. Study abroad participation in short-term programs (summer, January Term, or up to eight weeks in duration), has seen a 35.1% percentage increase since 1993/94. During the same period, there were declines in participation of 7.9% in mid-term programs, and 58.1% in long-term programs. In 2003/04, 93.5% of U.S. students studied abroad for one semester or less. Although short-term programs cannot provide students a deep exposure to the host destination's language and culture, they do allow more students to study abroad, especially those unable to spend a longer period of time abroad due to academic, financial, and other constraints.

Carnegie Category

The majority of students (51.6%) from all institutional types chose short-term study abroad programs over any other program duration, with the exception of students at Baccalaureate Institutions (the largest proportion of whom chose mid-term programs). About half of all students at the other institutional types studied abroad on short-term programs, with very few choosing long-term programs.

Fields of Study

The largest proportion (35.9%) of all U.S. students who studied abroad were majoring in the social sciences and humanities. Though social sciences and humanities majors still comprise the largest proportion of study abroad students, the percentage began to decline in 1991/92. Increasingly, study abroad students are business and management majors (17.7% in 2003/04). These majors, as well as mathematics, science, and engineering majors, have seen steady increases, while foreign language majors studying abroad have seen steady decreases since 1985/86. Most of the other majors have leveled off since 1998/99.

Profile of U.S. Students Abroad

While the destinations and the majors of U.S. students studying abroad have grown more diverse, the personal and academic characteristics of the students have remained relatively unchanged. As has been the case since the early days of study abroad, the "typical" study abroad student is Caucasian (83.7%) and female (65.6%). About a third (34.7%) was in their junior year of undergraduate study.

International students enrolled English Programs increased by in 2004, reversing four consecutive years of declines.

Rank	Place of Origin	2003 Total Students	2004 Total Students	2004 % of IEP Total Students	2004 % Change	2004 Student-Weeks
	WORLD TOTAL	**43,003**	**44,565**	-	**3.6**	**490,122**
1	Japan	10,519	10,804	24.2	2.7	113,358
2	Korea, Republic of	10,412	10,386	23.3	-0.2	127,591
3	Taiwan	4,235	5,126	11.5	21.0	54,774
4	Brazil	1,359	1,402	3.1	3.2	11,169
5	Turkey	1,034	1,133	2.5	9.6	11,776
6	France	1,156	1,093	2.5	-5.4	8,008
7	Thailand	943	1,088	2.4	15.4	11,998
8	China	796	1,026	2.3	28.9	11,891
9	Germany	849	950	2.1	11.9	7,622
10	Mexico	833	949	2.1	7.5	11,958
11	Italy	1,408	917	2.1	-34.9	4,917
12	Switzerland	732	729	1.6	-0.4	6,458
13	Spain	728	721	1.6	-1.0	5,348
14	Colombia	858	700	1.6	-18.4	8,777
15	Venezuela	742	648	1.5	-12.7	7,506
16	Hong Kong	130	366	0.8	181.5	5,158
17	Peru	269	342	0.8	27.1	3,783
18	Saudi Arabia	348	334	0.7	-4.0	4,586
19	Russia	273	296	0.7	8.4	2,785
20	Vietnam	245	292	0.7	19.2	4,578

The three leading places of origin, all in Asia, accounted for almost 60% of IEP enrollments in the U.S.

**n Intensive
.6% to 44,565**

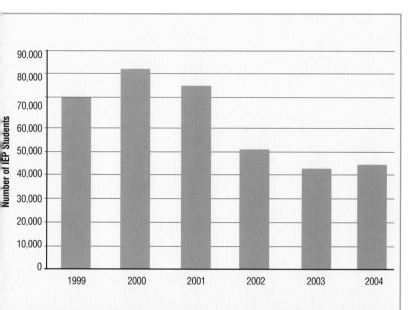

IEP enrollments increased, for the first time in four years, by 3.6% in 2004.

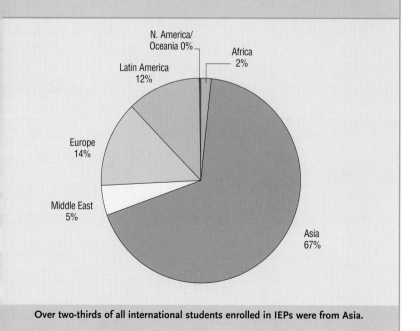

Over two-thirds of all international students enrolled in IEPs were from Asia.

After four consecutive years of declines, international student enrollment in Intensive English Programs (IEPs) increased slightly (3.6%) to 44,565 students in 2004. But enrollments remained substantially lower than the enrollment high of 85,238 in 2000, reached after a decade of strong growth. In addition, 2004 saw a decline in the number of student weeks to 490,122 (a decline of 1.2% from 2003), suggesting that more students were enrolled in IEPs for a shorter duration than in the past.

Japan remained the leading place of origin by total number of IEP students (10,804 or 24.2% of all IEP students), followed by Korea (10,386 or 23.3%), the leading place of origin by total student-weeks. These two places of origin alone comprised almost half (47.5%) of all IEP students. Only about half as many IEP students came from Taiwan (5,126 or 11.5%), the third leading place of origin. As with international student enrollments in U.S. degree programs, students from Asia were predominant among IEP enrollments, making up 67.4% of total IEP enrollments. Students from Europe were 13.5%, and students from Latin America were 11.9%. Among the leading 20 places of origin, seven were in Asia.

The IEP data is for the 2004 calendar year and is collected and reported by total headcount enrollment, as well as by student-weeks (one student studying for one week). The two variables together provide a fuller picture of IEP enrollments in the U.S.

89,634 international scholars were in the U.S. in 2004/05, an increase of 8.1% from the previous year.

Rank	Place of Origin	2003/04	2004/05	2004/05 % of U.S. Int'l Scholar Total	2004/05 % Change
	WORLD TOTAL	**82,905**	**89,634**	-	**8.1**
1	China	14,871	17,035	19.0	14.6
2	Korea, Republic of	7,290	8,301	9.3	13.9
3	India	6,809	7,755	8.7	13.9
4	Japan	5,627	5,62	6.3	-0.1
5	Germany	4,737	4,846	5.4	2.3
6	Canada	4,125	4,262	4.8	3.3
7	United Kingdom	3,117	3,185	3.6	2.2
8	France	2,842	3,078	3.4	8.3
9	Italy	2,317	2,565	2.9	10.7
10	Russia	2,403	2,420	2.7	0.7
11	Spain	1,893	2,043	2.3	7.9
12	Taiwan	1,347	1,543	1.7	14.6
13	Israel	1,409	1,500	1.7	6.5
14	Brazil	1,341	1,499	1.7	11.8
15	Turkey	1,215	1,427	1.6	17.4
16	Australia	1,197	1,183	1.3	-1.2
17	Mexico	1,032	1,158	1.3	12.2
18	Netherlands	975	946	1.1	-3.0
19	Poland	927	925	1.0	-0.2
20	Argentina	820	825	0.9	0.6

China, the leading place of origin, accounted for 19% of all international scholars in the U.S.

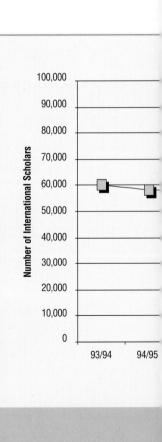

Leading Fields of Specialization	2004/05 % of Scholars
Health Sciences	21.9
Life & Biological Sciences	21.5
Physical Sciences	13.2
Engineering	11.6
Social Sciences & History	4.0
Agriculture	3.7
Computer & Information Sciences	3.1
Other	2.7
Business & Management	2.7
Mathematics	2.4
All Others	13.1
TOTAL	**89,634**

The sciences and engineering were the fields of specialization of 68% of international scholars in the U.S.

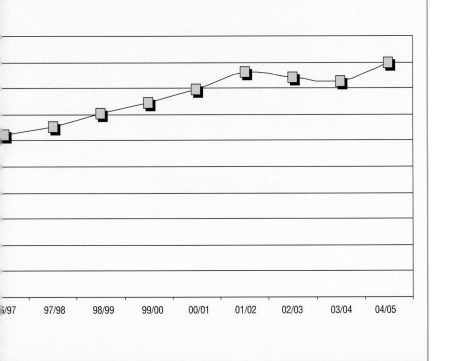

6/97	97/98	98/99	99/00	00/01	01/02	02/03	03/04	04/05

After two consecutive years of declines, the number of international scholars in the U.S. increased in 2004/05.

INTERNATIONAL SCHOLARS

In 2004/05, there was an 8.1% increase in the number of international scholars (89,634) at U.S. doctoral degree-granting institutions, which hosted the majority of visiting scholars in the U.S. This reverses two consecutive years of declines, which followed steady growth in the number of international scholars in the U.S. beginning in 1995/96.

China remained the leading place of origin, with 17,000 scholars, or 19.0% of the total. The leading four places of origin were all in Asia: China, Korea, India, and Japan; Germany was in fifth place. These leading five places of origin accounted for 48.6% of all international scholars in the U.S. International scholars from the leading 20 places of origin comprised 80.4% of the U.S. total, with almost all coming from Asia and Europe. Although there were eight European places of origin represented among the leading 20, the proportion of international scholars from Asia was much larger (48.7%) than from Europe (31.2%). Several places showed double-digit percentage increases from the previous year: China (14.6%), Korea (13.9%), India (13.9%), Italy (10.7%), Taiwan (14.6%), Brazil (11.8%), Turkey (17.4%), and Mexico (12.2%).

The majority of international scholars (68.2%) were teaching or conducting research in just four fields of specialization in the sciences and engineering – health sciences, life and biological sciences, physical sciences, and engineering. Almost three quarters (73.2%) were conducting research, and smaller proportions of scholars were teaching (13.3%), doing both (7.1%), or pursuing other activities (6.4%).

Global Competition
for International Enrollments

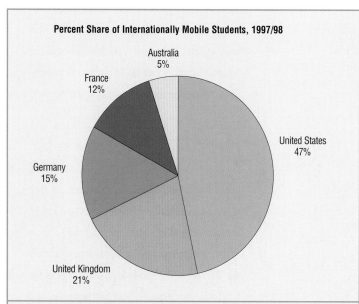

Percent Share of Internationally Mobile Students, 1997/98

Australia
5%

France
12%

Germany
15%

United Kingdom
21%

United States
47%

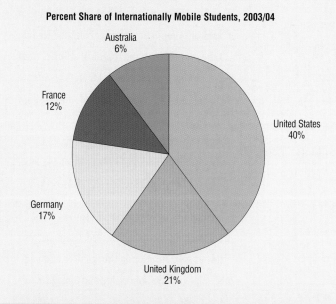

Percent Share of Internationally Mobile Students, 2003/04

Australia
6%

France
12%

Germany
17%

United Kingdom
21%

United States
40%

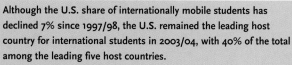

Although the U.S. share of internationally mobile students has declined 7% since 1997/98, the U.S. remained the leading host country for international students in 2003/04, with 40% of the total among the leading five host countries.

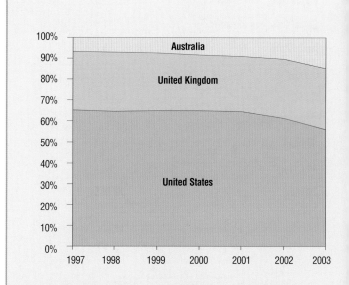

Australia

United Kingdom

United States

The drop in U.S. share is more pronounced among the leading three Anglophone host countries, down from 65% in 1997/98 to 56% in 2003/04. But international student enrollment in the U.S. remained almost twice as large as that of the next largest host country, with 572,509 international students enrolled on U.S. campuses in 2003/04 and 565,039 international students in 2004/05.

The data in these charts are from 2003/04, the most recently available statistics for all of the other leading host countries, with the exception of France (most recent data is from 2002/03). For an overview of international student mobility, see the *Atlas of Student Mobility* at *http://atlas.iienetwork.org*, a website of the Institute of International Education's Project Atlas and funded by the Ford Foundation.

INTERNATIONAL STUDENTS

IN THIS SECTION

TABLE	SOURCE	PAGE
Table 1	International Student Totals by Place of Origin, 2003/04 & 2004/05	26
Table 2	International Students by Academic Level and Place of Origin, 2004/05	29
Table 3	Enrollments in Metropolitan and Micropolitan Statistical Areas with More Than 1,000 International Students, 2004/05	35
Table 4	International Students in U.S. States and Regions, Selected Years 1969/70 – 2004/05	38
Table 5	International Students by Primary Source of Funds, 2003/04 & 2004/05	39
Table 6	Primary Source of Funds Within Academic Level, 2004/05	40
Table 7	International Student Enrollments by Institutional Type, 1999/00 – 2004/05	40
Table 8	Top 20 Places of Origin of International Students by Institutional Type, 2004/05	41
Table 9	International Students by Institutional Type: Top 40 Doctoral/Research Institutions, 2004/05	42
Table 10	International Students by Institutional Type: Top 40 Master's Institutions, 2004/05	43
Table 11	International Students by Institutional Type: Top 40 Baccalaureate Institutions, 2004/05	44
Table 12	International Students By Institutional Type: Top 40 Associate's Institutions, 2004/05	45
Table 13	International Students By Institutional Type: Top 40 Specialized Institutions, 2004/05	46
Table 14	Institutions with 1,000 or More International Students: Ranked by International Student Total, 2004/05	47
Table 15	International Students by Field of Study, 2003/04 & 2004/05	50
Table 16	Fields of Study by Institutional Type, 2004/05	52
Table 17	International Students by Academic Level, 2003/04 & 2004/05	53
Table 18	International Students by Academic Level, Selected Years 1954/55 – 2004/05	54
Table 19	Personal and Academic Characteristics of International Students by Academic Level, 2004/05	55
Table 20	Personal Characteristics of International Students, 1976/77 – 2004/05	56

Place of Origin	2003/04	2004/05	% Change
AFRICA	**38,150**	**36,100**	**-5.4**
Africa, Unspecified	1	0	-100.0
East Africa	**14,831**	**13,675**	**-7.8**
Burundi	80	82	2.5
Comoros	22	23	4.5
Djibouti	2	5	150.0
Eritrea	127	194	52.8
Ethiopia	1,060	1,129	6.5
Kenya	7,381	6,728	-8.8
Madagascar	109	127	16.5
Malawi	399	375	-6.0
Mauritius	209	188	-10.0
Mozambique	93	106	14.0
Reunion	2	8	300.0
Rwanda	275	191	-30.5
Seychelles	10	10	0.0
Somalia	37	55	48.6
Tanzania	1,471	1,332	-9.4
Uganda	696	632	-9.2
Zambia	859	794	-7.6
Zimbabwe	1,999	1,695	-15.2
East Africa, Unspecified	0	1	-
Central Africa	**2,331**	**2,505**	**7.5**
Angola	442	431	-2.5
Cameroon	1,216	1,364	12.2
Central African Republic	40	32	-20.0
Chad	95	75	-21.1
Congo	9	23	155.6
Congo (Former Zaire)	340	323	-5.0
Equatorial Guinea	79	104	31.6
Gabon	105	145	38.1
São Tomé & Príncipe	5	8	60.0
North Africa	**4,487**	**3,898**	**-13.1**
Algeria	148	143	-3.4
Egypt	1,822	1,574	-13.6
Libya	39	39	0.0
Morocco	1,835	1,571	-14.4
Sudan	279	290	3.9
Tunisia	341	268	-21.4
Western Sahara	23	13	-43.5
North Africa, Unspecified	0	0	-

Place of Origin	2003/04	2004/05	% Change
Southern Africa	**2,679**	**2,240**	**-16.4**
Botswana	488	338	-30.7
Lesotho	39	41	5.1
Namibia	95	66	-30.5
South Africa	1,971	1,699	-13.8
Swaziland	86	96	11.6
West Africa	**13,821**	**13,782**	**-0.3**
Benin	168	180	7.1
Burkina Faso	191	277	45.0
Cape Verde	52	40	-23.1
Côte d'Ivoire	636	622	-2.2
Gambia	523	445	-14.9
Ghana	3,288	3,114	-5.3
Guinea	250	225	-10.0
Guinea-Bissau	16	11	-31.3
Liberia	411	343	-16.5
Mali	378	345	-8.7
Mauritania	68	58	-14.7
Niger	169	234	38.5
Nigeria	6,140	6,335	3.2
Senegal	805	725	-9.9
Sierra Leone	306	308	0.7
St. Helena	1	1	0.0
Togo	413	514	24.5
West Africa, Unspecified	6	5	-16.7
ASIA	**324,006**	**325,112**	**0.3**
East Asia	**189,874**	**192,561**	**1.4**
China	61,765	62,523	1.2
Hong Kong	7,353	7,180	-2.4
Japan	40,835	42,215	3.4
Korea, Dem. People's Rep.	174	219	25.9
Korea, Republic of	52,484	53,358	1.7
Macau	374	383	2.4
Mongolia	711	769	8.2
Taiwan	26,178	25,914	-1.0
South & Central Asia	**98,138**	**97,961**	**-0.2**
Afghanistan	109	155	42.2
Bangladesh	3,198	2,758	-13.8
Bhutan	63	70	11.1
India	79,736	80,466	0.9
Kazakhstan	538	477	-11.3

1   INTERNATIONAL STUDENT TOTALS BY PLACE OF ORIGIN, 2003/04 & 2004/05

Place of Origin	2003/04	2004/05	% Change	Place of Origin	2003/04	2004/05	% Change
Kyrgyzstan	179	185	3.4	Belarus	422	431	2.1
Nepal	4,384	4,861	10.9	Bosnia & Herzegovina	433	359	-17.1
Pakistan	7,325	6,296	-14.0	Bulgaria	3,734	3,644	-2.4
Maldives	15	24	60.0	Croatia	660	675	2.3
Sri Lanka	1,964	1,992	1.4	Czech Republic	1,052	902	-14.3
Tajikistan	117	158	35.0	Czechoslovakia, Former	7	81	1,057.1
Turkmenistan	98	103	5.1	Estonia	271	283	4.4
Uzbekistan	412	416	1.0	Georgia	373	340	-8.8
				Hungary	997	934	-6.3
Southeast Asia	**35,994**	**34,590**	**-3.9**	Kosovo	0	35	-
Brunei	13	18	38.5	Latvia	424	408	-3.8
Cambodia	330	333	0.9	Lithuania	691	635	-8.1
East Timor	8	16	100.0	Macedonia	349	381	9.2
Indonesia	8,880	7,760	-12.6	Moldova	266	285	7.1
Laos	65	63	-3.1	Poland	2,913	2,861	-1.8
Malaysia	6,483	6,142	-5.3	Romania	3,320	3,217	-3.1
Myanmar	691	651	-5.8	Russia	5,532	5,073	-8.3
Philippines	3,467	3,531	1.8	Serbia & Montenegro/Kosovo	0	391	-
Singapore	3,955	3,769	-4.7	Slovakia	585	609	4.1
Thailand	8,937	8,637	-3.4	Slovenia	209	306	46.4
Vietnam	3,165	3,670	16.0	Ukraine	2,004	1,831	-8.6
				U.S.S.R., Former	50	111	122.0
MIDDLE EAST	**31,852**	**31,248**	**-1.9**	Yugoslavia, Former	1,851	1,233	-33.4
Bahrain	444	377	-15.1	E. Europe, Unspecified	1	0	-100.0
Cyprus	1,562	1,326	-15.1				
Iran	2,321	2,251	-3.0	**Western Europe**	**46,424**	**45,056**	**-2.9**
Iraq	120	142	18.3	Andorra	9	11	22.2
Israel	3,474	3,323	-4.3	Austria	899	885	-1.6
Jordan	1,853	1,754	-5.3	Belgium	823	743	-9.7
Kuwait	1,846	1,720	-6.8	Denmark	859	887	3.3
Lebanon	2,179	2,040	-6.4	Finland	619	570	-7.9
Oman	445	354	-20.4	France	6,818	6,555	-3.9
Palestinian Authority	247	268	8.5	Germany	8,745	8,640	-1.2
Qatar	354	290	-18.1	Gibraltar	0	9	-
Saudi Arabia	3,521	3,035	-13.8	Greece	2,126	2,035	-4.3
Syria	556	498	-10.4	Iceland	488	434	-11.1
Turkey	11,398	12,474	9.4	Ireland	1,020	976	-4.3
United Arab Emirates	1,248	1,158	-7.2	Italy	3,308	3,261	-1.4
Yemen	284	238	-16.2	Liechtenstein	6	9	50.0
				Luxembourg	50	39	-22.0
EUROPE	**74,134**	**71,609**	**-3.4**	Malta	30	27	-10.0
				Monaco	8	9	12.5
Eastern Europe	**27,710**	**26,553**	**-4.2**	Netherlands	1,505	1,474	-2.1
Albania	916	866	-5.5	Norway	1,471	1,414	-3.9
Armenia	412	410	-0.5	Portugal	880	852	-3.2
Azerbaijan	238	252	5.9	San Marino	2	3	50.0

1 (cont'd) INTERNATIONAL STUDENT TOTALS BY PLACE OF ORIGIN, 2003/04 & 2004/05

Place of Origin	2003/04	2004/05	% Change	Place of Origin	2003/04	2004/05	% Change
Spain	3,631	3,512	-3.3	Argentina	3,644	3,363	-7.7
Sweden	3,116	3,106	-0.3	Bolivia	1,004	1,008	0.4
Switzerland	1,561	1,361	-12.8	Brazil	7,799	7,244	-7.1
United Kingdom	8,439	8,236	-2.4	Chile	1,612	3,290	104.1
Vatican City	11	8	-27.3	Colombia	7,533	7,334	-2.6
				Ecuador	2,345	2,177	-7.2
LATIN AMERICA	**69,658**	**67,818**	**-2.6**	Falkland Islands	0	0	-
				French Guiana	1	3	200.0
Caribbean	**15,606**	**13,898**	**-10.9**	Guyana	503	441	-12.3
Anguilla	62	61	-1.6	Paraguay	343	305	-11.1
Antigua	240	204	-15.0	Peru	3,771	3,631	-3.7
Aruba	60	70	16.7	Suriname	126	92	-27.0
Bahamas	2,030	1,638	-19.3	Uruguay	532	526	-1.1
Barbados	569	494	-13.2	Venezuela	5,575	5,279	-5.3
British Virgin Islands	145	187	29.0				
Cayman Islands	191	168	-12.0	**NORTH AMERICA**	**27,650**	**28,634**	**3.6**
Cuba	132	190	43.9	Bermuda	633	494	-22.0
Dominica	232	319	37.5	Canada	27,017	28,140	4.2
Dominican Republic	998	868	-13.0				
Grenada	229	210	-8.3	**OCEANIA**	**4,534**	**4,481**	**-1.2**
Guadeloupe	5	10	100.0	Australia	2,706	2,659	-1.7
Haiti	1,074	1,002	-6.7	Cook Islands	3	3	0.0
Jamaica	4,994	4,368	-12.5	Fed. States of Micronesia	182	128	-29.7
Martinique	9	16	77.8	Fiji	177	184	4.0
Montserrat	6	13	116.7	French Polynesia	97	91	-6.2
Netherlands Antilles	225	203	-9.8	Kiribati	53	32	-39.6
St. Kitts-Nevis	167	196	17.4	Marshall Islands	24	91	279.2
St. Lucia	299	345	15.4	Nauru	0	8	-
St. Vincent	183	175	-4.4	New Caledonia	9	9	0.0
Trinidad & Tobago	3,638	2,930	-19.5	New Zealand	962	900	-6.4
Turks & Caicos Islands	78	168	115.4	Niue	11	6	-45.5
Windward Islands	0	0	-	Norfolk Island	0	0	-
Caribbean, Unspecified	40	63	57.5	Palau	45	38	-15.6
				Papua New Guinea	32	35	9.4
Central America & Mexico	**19,264**	**19,227**	**-0.2**	Solomon Islands	9	19	111.1
Belize	501	449	-10.4	Tonga	111	146	31.5
Costa Rica	907	895	-1.3	Tuvalu	5	1	-80.0
El Salvador	976	962	-1.4	Vanuatu	5	7	40.0
Guatemala	1,030	1,037	0.7	Wallis & Futuna Isles	0	1	-
Honduras	1,089	1,140	4.7	Western Samoa	103	123	19.4
Mexico	13,329	13,063	-2.0				
Nicaragua	473	673	42.3	**STATELESS**	**19**	**37**	**94.7**
Panama	958	1,008	5.2				
C. America & Mexico, Unspec.	1	0	-100.0	**UNKNOWN**	**2,506**	**-**	**-**
South America	**34,788**	**34,693**	**-0.3**	**WORLD TOTAL**	**572,509**	**565,039**	**-1.3**

1 (cont'd) INTERNATIONAL STUDENT TOTALS BY PLACE OF ORIGIN, 2003/04 & 2004/05

Place of Origin	Under-graduate	% Under-graduate	Graduate	% Graduate	Other	% Other	Total
AFRICA	**22,753**	**63.0**	**11,439**	**31.7**	**1,908**	**5.3**	**36,100**
Africa, Unspecified	0	-	0	-	0	-	0
East Africa	**9,029**	**66.0**	**4,054**	**29.6**	**592**	**4.3**	**13,675**
Burundi	58	70.7	16	19.5	8	9.8	82
Comoros	19	82.6	4	17.4	0	0.0	23
Djibouti	4	80.0	1	20.0	0	0.0	5
Eritrea	67	34.5	122	62.9	5	2.6	194
Ethiopia	625	55.4	448	39.7	56	5.0	1,129
Kenya	4,607	68.5	1,856	27.6	265	3.9	6,728
Madagascar	57	44.9	58	45.7	12	9.4	127
Malawi	260	69.3	101	26.9	14	3.7	375
Mauritius	127	67.6	52	27.7	9	4.8	188
Mozambique	51	48.1	55	51.9	0	0.0	106
Reunion	8	100.0	0	0.0	0	0.0	8
Rwanda	124	64.9	63	33.0	4	2.1	191
Seychelles	5	50.0	5	50.0	0	0.0	10
Somalia	36	65.5	15	27.3	4	7.3	55
Tanzania	881	66.1	377	28.3	74	5.6	1,332
Uganda	318	50.3	286	45.3	28	4.4	632
Zambia	570	71.8	192	24.2	32	4.0	794
Zimbabwe	1,211	71.4	403	23.8	81	4.8	1,695
East Africa, Unspecified	1	100.0	0	0.0	0	0.0	1
Central Africa	**1,784**	**71.2**	**616**	**24.6**	**105**	**4.2**	**2,505**
Angola	317	73.5	84	19.5	30	7.0	431
Cameroon	943	69.1	383	28.1	38	2.8	1,364
Central African Republic	23	71.9	6	18.8	3	9.4	32
Chad	44	58.7	22	29.3	9	12.0	75
Congo	17	73.9	6	26.1	0	0.0	23
Congo (Former Zaire)	237	73.4	75	23.2	11	3.4	323
Equatorial Guinea	91	87.5	10	9.6	3	2.9	104
Gabon	107	73.8	27	18.6	11	7.6	145
São Tomé & Príncipe	5	62.5	3	37.5	0	0.0	8
North Africa	**1,693**	**43.4**	**1,918**	**49.2**	**287**	**7.4**	**3,898**
Algeria	60	42.0	69	48.3	14	9.8	143
Egypt	411	26.1	1,077	68.4	86	5.5	1,574
Libya	29	74.4	9	23.1	1	2.6	39
Morocco	908	57.8	542	34.5	121	7.7	1,571
Sudan	156	53.8	101	34.8	33	11.4	290
Tunisia	120	44.8	116	43.3	32	11.9	268
Western Sahara	9	69.2	4	30.8	0	0.0	13
Southern Africa	**1,327**	**59.2**	**796**	**35.5**	**117**	**5.2**	**2,240**

2 INTERNATIONAL STUDENTS BY ACADEMIC LEVEL AND PLACE OF ORIGIN, 2004/05

Place of Origin	Under-graduate	% Under-graduate	Graduate	% Graduate	Other	% Other	Total
Botswana	174	51.5	150	44.4	14	4.1	338
Lesotho	28	68.3	13	31.7	0	0.0	41
Namibia	36	54.5	30	45.5	0	0.0	66
South Africa	1,024	60.3	576	33.9	99	5.8	1,699
Swaziland	65	67.7	27	28.1	4	4.2	96
West Africa	**8,920**	**64.7**	**4,055**	**29.4**	**807**	**5.9**	**13,782**
Benin	118	65.6	48	26.7	14	7.8	180
Burkina Faso	181	65.3	77	27.8	19	6.9	277
Cape Verde	32	80.0	5	12.5	3	7.5	40
Côte d'Ivoire	401	64.5	161	25.9	60	9.6	622
Gambia	387	87.0	47	10.6	11	2.5	445
Ghana	1,674	53.8	1,258	40.4	182	5.8	3,114
Guinea	156	69.3	36	16.0	33	14.7	225
Guinea-Bissau	9	81.8	2	18.2	0	0.0	11
Liberia	247	72.0	87	25.4	9	2.6	343
Mali	236	68.4	79	22.9	30	8.7	345
Mauritania	39	67.2	11	19.0	8	13.8	58
Niger	141	60.3	66	28.2	27	11.5	234
Nigeria	4,276	67.5	1,778	28.1	281	4.4	6,335
Senegal	485	66.9	183	25.2	57	7.9	725
Sierra Leone	194	63.0	99	32.1	15	4.9	308
St. Helena	1	100.0	0	0.0	0	0.0	1
Togo	341	66.3	115	22.4	58	11.3	514
West Africa, Unspecified	2	40.0	3	60.0	0	0.0	5
ASIA	**120,272**	**37.0**	**175,714**	**54.0**	**29,126**	**9.0**	**325,112**
East Asia	**74,557**	**38.7**	**98,481**	**51.1**	**19,523**	**10.1**	**192,561**
China	8,299	13.3	49,293	78.8	4,931	7.9	62,523
Hong Kong	5,226	72.8	1,449	20.2	505	7.0	7,180
Japan	28,708	68.0	8,497	20.1	5,010	11.9	42,215
Korea, Dem. People's Rep.	168	76.7	45	20.5	6	2.7	219
Korea, Republic of	23,432	43.9	24,122	45.2	5,804	10.9	53,358
Macau	304	79.4	57	14.9	22	5.7	383
Mongolia	491	63.8	192	25.0	86	11.2	769
Taiwan	7,929	30.6	14,826	57.2	3,159	12.2	25,914
South & Central Asia	**26,423**	**27.0**	**64,381**	**65.7**	**7,157**	**7.3**	**97,961**
Afghanistan	90	58.1	27	17.4	38	24.5	155
Bangladesh	1,238	44.9	1,312	47.6	208	7.5	2,758
Bhutan	38	54.3	31	44.3	1	1.4	70
India	16,443	20.4	57,976	72.1	6,047	7.5	80,466
Kazakhstan	237	49.7	200	41.9	40	8.4	477
Kyrgyzstan	91	49.2	83	44.9	11	5.9	185

2   (cont'd) INTERNATIONAL STUDENTS BY ACADEMIC LEVEL AND PLACE OF ORIGIN, 2004/05

Place of Origin	Under-graduate	% Under-graduate	Graduate	% Graduate	Other	% Other	Total
Maldives	15	62.5	7	29.2	2	8.3	24
Nepal	3,217	66.2	1,427	29.4	217	4.5	4,861
Pakistan	3,758	59.7	2,096	33.3	442	7.0	6,296
Sri Lanka	948	47.6	963	48.3	81	4.1	1,992
Tajikistan	81	51.3	47	29.7	30	19.0	158
Turkmenistan	56	54.4	43	41.7	4	3.9	103
Uzbekistan	211	50.7	169	40.6	36	8.7	416
Southeast Asia	**19,292**	**55.8**	**12,852**	**37.2**	**2,446**	**7.1**	**34,590**
Brunei	13	72.2	4	22.2	1	5.6	18
Cambodia	233	70.0	69	20.7	31	9.3	333
East Timor	7	43.8	8	50.0	1	6.3	16
Indonesia	5,227	67.4	2,021	26.0	512	6.6	7,760
Laos	45	71.4	11	17.5	7	11.1	63
Malaysia	4,286	69.8	1,534	25.0	322	5.2	6,142
Myanmar	452	69.4	156	24.0	43	6.6	651
Philippines	2,037	57.7	1,277	36.2	217	6.1	3,531
Singapore	2,104	55.8	1,393	37.0	272	7.2	3,769
Thailand	2,459	28.5	5,282	61.2	896	10.4	8,637
Vietnam	2,429	66.2	1,097	29.9	144	3.9	3,670
MIDDLE EAST	**14,284**	**45.7**	**14,727**	**47.1**	**2,237**	**7.2**	**31,248**
Bahrain	269	71.4	94	24.9	14	3.7	377
Cyprus	695	52.4	544	41.0	87	6.6	1,326
Iran	652	29.0	1,475	65.5	124	5.5	2,251
Iraq	66	46.5	57	40.1	19	13.4	142
Israel	1,383	41.6	1,653	49.7	287	8.6	3,323
Jordan	568	32.4	1,079	61.5	107	6.1	1,754
Kuwait	1,197	69.6	398	23.1	125	7.3	1,720
Lebanon	889	43.6	1,019	50.0	132	6.5	2,040
Oman	220	62.1	105	29.7	29	8.2	354
Palestinian Authority	114	42.5	136	50.7	18	6.7	268
Qatar	249	85.9	31	10.7	10	3.4	290
Saudi Arabia	1,700	56.0	1,084	35.7	251	8.3	3,035
Syria	222	44.6	217	43.6	59	11.8	498
Turkey	5,079	40.7	6,535	52.4	860	6.9	12,474
United Arab Emirates	858	74.1	212	18.3	88	7.6	1,158
Yemen	123	51.7	88	37.0	27	11.3	238
EUROPE	**32,508**	**45.4**	**31,393**	**43.8**	**7,708**	**10.8**	**71,609**
Eastern Europe	**12,680**	**47.8**	**12,100**	**45.6**	**1,773**	**6.7**	**26,553**
Albania	525	60.6	288	33.3	53	6.1	866
Armenia	168	41.0	219	53.4	23	5.6	410
Azerbaijan	100	39.7	126	50.0	26	10.3	252

2 (cont'd) INTERNATIONAL STUDENTS BY ACADEMIC LEVEL AND PLACE OF ORIGIN, 2004/05

Place of Origin	Under- graduate	% Under- graduate	Graduate	% Graduate	Other	% Other	Total
Belarus	210	48.7	184	42.7	37	8.6	431
Bosnia & Herzegovina	244	68.0	102	28.4	13	3.6	359
Bulgaria	2,109	57.9	1,337	36.7	198	5.4	3,644
Croatia	336	49.8	290	43.0	49	7.3	675
Czech Republic	469	52.0	334	37.0	99	11.0	902
Czechoslovakia, Former	30	37.0	20	24.7	31	38.3	81
Estonia	168	59.4	107	37.8	8	2.8	283
Georgia	128	37.6	188	55.3	24	7.1	340
Hungary	436	46.7	414	44.3	84	9.0	934
Kosovo	25	71.4	6	17.1	4	11.4	35
Latvia	259	63.5	119	29.2	30	7.4	408
Lithuania	401	63.1	200	31.5	34	5.4	635
Macedonia	183	48.0	181	47.5	17	4.5	381
Moldova	156	54.7	110	38.6	19	6.7	285
Poland	1,739	60.8	948	33.1	174	6.1	2,861
Romania	893	27.8	2,163	67.2	161	5.0	3,217
Russia	1,997	39.4	2,662	52.5	414	8.2	5,073
Serbia & Montenegro/Kosovo	164	41.9	197	50.4	30	7.7	391
Slovakia	333	54.7	231	37.9	45	7.4	609
Slovenia	185	60.5	102	33.3	19	6.2	306
Ukraine	680	37.1	1,040	56.8	111	6.1	1,831
U.S.S.R., Former	90	81.1	18	16.2	3	2.7	111
Yugoslavia, Former	652	52.9	514	41.7	67	5.4	1,233
Western Europe	**19,828**	**44.0**	**19,293**	**42.8**	**5,935**	**13.2**	**45,056**
Andorra	7	63.6	3	27.3	1	9.1	11
Austria	418	47.2	344	38.9	123	13.9	885
Belgium	282	38.0	391	52.6	70	9.4	743
Denmark	412	46.4	292	32.9	183	20.6	887
Finland	309	54.2	181	31.8	80	14.0	570
France	2,458	37.5	3,064	46.7	1,033	15.8	6,555
Germany	3,558	41.2	3,811	44.1	1,271	14.7	8,640
Gibraltar	8	88.9	1	11.1	0	0.0	9
Greece	475	23.3	1,395	68.6	165	8.1	2,035
Iceland	173	39.9	239	55.1	22	5.1	434
Ireland	469	48.1	417	42.7	90	9.2	976
Italy	876	26.9	1,938	59.4	447	13.7	3,261
Liechtenstein	2	22.2	6	66.7	1	11.1	9
Luxembourg	14	35.9	23	59.0	2	5.1	39
Malta	7	25.9	14	51.9	6	22.2	27
Monaco	5	55.6	3	33.3	1	11.1	9
Netherlands	740	50.2	526	35.7	208	14.1	1,474
Norway	810	57.3	451	31.9	153	10.8	1,414
Portugal	324	38.0	457	53.6	71	8.3	852
San Marino	2	66.7	1	33.3	0	0.0	3

2   (cont'd) INTERNATIONAL STUDENTS BY ACADEMIC LEVEL AND PLACE OF ORIGIN, 2004/05

Place of Origin	Under-graduate	% Under-graduate	Graduate	% Graduate	Other	% Other	Total
Spain	1,216	34.6	1,767	50.3	529	15.1	3,512
Sweden	2,180	70.2	623	20.1	303	9.8	3,106
Switzerland	609	44.7	559	41.1	193	14.2	1,361
United Kingdom	4,471	54.3	2,785	33.8	980	11.9	8,236
Vatican City	3	37.5	2	25.0	3	37.5	8
LATIN AMERICA	**40,778**	**60.1**	**21,967**	**32.4**	**5,073**	**7.5**	**67,818**
Caribbean	**9,977**	**71.8**	**3,210**	**23.1**	**711**	**5.1**	**13,898**
Anguilla	49	80.3	10	16.4	2	3.3	61
Antigua	158	77.5	36	17.6	10	4.9	204
Aruba	55	78.6	11	15.7	4	5.7	70
Bahamas	1,242	75.8	329	20.1	67	4.1	1,638
Barbados	294	59.5	171	34.6	29	5.9	494
British Virgin Islands	157	84.0	26	13.9	4	2.1	187
Cayman Islands	139	82.7	25	14.9	4	2.4	168
Cuba	151	79.5	28	14.7	11	5.8	190
Dominica	222	69.6	88	27.6	9	2.8	319
Dominican Republic	560	64.5	233	26.8	75	8.6	868
Grenada	152	72.4	50	23.8	8	3.8	210
Guadeloupe	7	70.0	1	10.0	2	20.0	10
Haiti	803	80.1	141	14.1	58	5.8	1,002
Jamaica	3,036	69.5	1,082	24.8	250	5.7	4,368
Martinique	11	68.8	5	31.3	0	0.0	16
Montserrat	7	53.8	6	46.2	0	0.0	13
Netherlands Antilles	166	81.8	26	12.8	11	5.4	203
St. Kitts-Nevis	136	69.4	53	27.0	7	3.6	196
St. Lucia	243	70.4	90	26.1	12	3.5	345
St. Vincent	141	80.6	29	16.6	5	2.9	175
Trinidad & Tobago	2,082	71.1	714	24.4	134	4.6	2,930
Turks & Caicos Islands	133	79.2	31	18.5	4	2.4	168
Caribbean, Unspecified	33	52.4	25	39.7	5	7.9	63
Central America & Mexico	**12,543**	**65.2**	**5,452**	**28.4**	**1,232**	**6.4**	**19,227**
Belize	270	60.1	151	33.6	28	6.2	449
Costa Rica	446	49.8	401	44.8	48	5.4	895
El Salvador	751	78.1	156	16.2	55	5.7	962
Guatemala	743	71.6	235	22.7	59	5.7	1,037
Honduras	873	76.6	213	18.7	54	4.7	1,140
Mexico	8,200	62.8	3,961	30.3	902	6.9	13,063
Nicaragua	549	81.6	90	13.4	34	5.1	673
Panama	711	70.5	245	24.3	52	5.2	1,008
South America	**18,258**	**52.6**	**13,305**	**38.4**	**3,130**	**9.0**	**34,693**
Argentina	1,245	37.0	1,807	53.7	311	9.2	3,363

2   (cont'd) INTERNATIONAL STUDENTS BY ACADEMIC LEVEL AND PLACE OF ORIGIN, 2004/05

Place of Origin	Under-graduate	% Under-graduate	Graduate	% Graduate	Other	% Other	Total
Bolivia	668	66.3	268	26.6	72	7.1	1,008
Brazil	3,755	51.8	2,814	38.8	675	9.3	7,244
Chile	1,185	36.0	1,712	52.0	393	11.9	3,290
Colombia	3,911	53.3	2,727	37.2	696	9.5	7,334
Ecuador	1,428	65.6	591	27.1	158	7.3	2,177
French Guiana	3	100.0	0	0.0	0	0.0	3
Guyana	338	76.6	87	19.7	16	3.6	441
Paraguay	202	66.2	74	24.3	29	9.5	305
Peru	1,961	54.0	1,396	38.4	274	7.5	3,631
Suriname	58	63.0	30	32.6	4	4.3	92
Uruguay	208	39.5	277	52.7	41	7.8	526
Venezuela	3,296	62.4	1,522	28.8	461	8.7	5,279
NORTH AMERICA	**14,091**	**49.2**	**13,180**	**46.0**	**1,363**	**4.8**	**28,634**
Bermuda	381	77.1	93	18.8	20	4.0	494
Canada	13,710	48.7	13,087	46.5	1,343	4.8	28,140
OCEANIA	**2,552**	**57.0**	**1,493**	**33.3**	**436**	**9.7**	**4,481**
Australia	1,387	52.2	965	36.3	307	11.5	2,659
Cook Islands	2	66.7	1	33.3	0	0.0	3
Fed. States of Micronesia	122	95.3	3	2.3	3	2.3	128
Fiji	151	82.1	23	12.5	10	5.4	184
French Polynesia	85	93.4	6	6.6	0	0.0	91
Kiribati	28	87.5	3	9.4	1	3.1	32
Marshall Islands	90	98.9	1	1.1	0	0.0	91
Nauru	5	62.5	3	37.5	0	0.0	8
New Caledonia	6	66.7	3	33.3	0	0.0	9
New Zealand	401	44.6	438	48.7	61	6.8	900
Niue	3	50.0	3	50.0	0	0.0	6
Palau	33	86.8	5	13.2	0	0.0	38
Papua New Guinea	23	65.7	10	28.6	2	5.7	35
Solomon Islands	15	78.9	4	21.1	0	0.0	19
Tonga	113	77.4	10	6.8	23	15.8	146
Tuvalu	0	0.0	1	100.0	0	0.0	1
Vanuatu	6	85.7	1	14.3	0	0.0	7
Wallis & Futuna Isles	1	100.0	0	0.0	0	0.0	1
Western Samoa	81	65.9	13	10.6	29	23.6	123
STATELESS	**17**	**45.9**	**20**	**54.1**	**0**	**0.0**	**37**
UNKNOWN	-	-	-	-	-	-	**0**
WORLD TOTAL*	**247,255**	**43.8**	**269,933**	**47.8**	**47,851**	**8.5**	**565,039**

* Academic level totals by place of origin differ from the official academic level totals reported in Table 18 and throughout, due to the difference in responses from some of the institutions to the nationality and academic level survey questions.

2 (cont'd) INTERNATIONAL STUDENTS BY ACADEMIC LEVEL AND PLACE OF ORIGIN, 2004/05

Rank	Metropolitan/Micropolitan Statistical Area * **	Int'l Students
1	New York-Newark-Edison, NY-NJ-PA	49,470
2	Los Angeles-Long Beach-Santa Ana, CA	33,736
3	Boston-Cambridge-Quincy, MA-NH	23,336
4	Washington-Arlington-Alexandria, DC-VA-MD-WV	18,811
5	Chicago-Naperville-Joliet, IL-IN-WI	14,757
6	San Francisco-Oakland-Fremont, CA	13,783
7	Dallas-Fort Worth-Arlington, TX	13,611
8	Philadelphia-Camden-Wilmington, PA-NJ-DE-MD	12,707
9	Houston-Baytown-Sugar Land, TX	11,707
10	Miami-Fort Lauderdale-Miami Beach, FL	11,177
Total of Top 10		**203,095**
11	San Jose-Sunnyvale-Santa Clara, CA	8,965
12	Atlanta-Sandy Springs-Marietta, GA	8,348
13	Seattle-Tacoma-Bellevue, WA	7,503
14	Austin-Round Rock, TX	6,776
15	Buffalo-Cheektowaga-Tonawanda, NY	6,303
16	Phoenix-Mesa-Scottsdale, AZ	5,928
17	San Diego-Carlsbad-San Marcos, CA	5,886
18	Champaign-Urbana, IL	5,858
19	Baltimore-Towson, MD	5,614
20	Ann Arbor, MI	5,608
21	Pittsburgh, PA	5,504
22	Detroit-Warren-Livonia, MI	5,455
23	Columbus, OH	5,306
24	Minneapolis-St. Paul-Bloomington, MN-WI	5,294
25	Lafayette, IN	4,939
26	Honolulu, HI	4,826
27	St. Louis, MO-IL	4,417
28	Oklahoma City, OK	4,245
29	Madison, WI	4,056
30	Lansing-East Lansing, MI	3,845
31	Gainesville, FL	3,835
32	College Station-Bryan, TX	3,721
33	Tucson, AZ	3,598
34	Durham, NC	3,540
35	Bloomington, IN	3,525
36	Ithaca, NY	3,458
37	Providence-New Bedford-Fall River, RI-MA	3,433
38	State College, PA	3,237
39	Tampa-St. Petersburg-Clearwater, FL	3,146
40	Orlando, FL	3,047
41	Riverside-San Bernardino-Ontario, CA	3,015
42	Sacramento—Arden-Arcade—Roseville, CA	3,012
43	Hartford-West Hartford-East Hartford, CT	2,955
44	Rochester, NY	2,904

3 ENROLLMENTS IN METROPOLITAN AND MICROPOLITAN STATISTICAL AREAS WITH MORE THAN 1,000 INTERNATIONAL STUDENTS, 2004/05

Rank	Metropolitan/Micropolitan Statistical Area * **	Int'l Students
45	Cincinnati-Middletown, OH-KY-IN	2,723
45	Syracuse, NY	2,723
47	Provo-Orem, UT	2,707
48	Denver-Aurora, CO	2,623
49	El Paso, TX	2,588
50	Springfield, MA	2,529
51	Albany-Schenectady-Troy, NY	2,439
52	Cleveland-Elyria-Mentor, OH	2,432
53	Iowa City, IA	2,373
54	New Orleans-Metairie-Kenner, LA	2,355
55	Ames, IA	2,295
56	New Haven-Milford, CT	2,280
57	Salt Lake City, UT	2,247
58	Blacksburg-Christiansburg-Radford, VA	2,238
59	Portland-Vancouver-Beaverton, OR-WA	2,147
60	Stillwater, OK Micropolitan Statistical Area	1,999
61	Las Vegas-Paradise, NV	1,978
62	Baton Rouge, LA	1,975
63	Raleigh-Cary, NC	1,964
64	Virginia Beach-Norfolk-Newport News, VA-NC	1,881
65	Milwaukee-Waukesha-West Allis, WI	1,866
66	Omaha-Council Bluffs, NE-IA	1,847
67	Kansas City, MO-KS	1,787
68	San Antonio, TX	1,768
69	Tallahassee, FL	1,752
70	Charlottesville, VA	1,743
71	Lexington-Fayette, KY	1,734
72	Akron, OH	1,702
73	Wichita, KS	1,696
74	Bridgeport-Stamford-Norwalk, CT	1,672
75	Eugene-Springfield, OR	1,664
76	Columbia, MO	1,650
77	Toledo, OH	1,645
78	Santa Barbara-Santa Maria-Goleta, CA	1,637
79	Lawrence, KS	1,626
80	Kalamazoo-Portage, MI	1,599
81	Nashville-Davidson—Murfreesboro, TN	1,577
82	Pullman, WA Micropolitan Statistical Area	1,545
83	Lincoln, NE	1,543
84	Carbondale, IL Micropolitan Statistical Area	1,542
85	Trenton-Ewing, NJ	1,515
86	Athens, OH Micropolitan Statistical Area	1,472
87	Memphis, TN-MS-AR	1,461
88	Worcester, MA	1,438
89	Binghamton, NY	1,395
90	South Bend-Mishawaka, IN-MI	1,341

3 (cont'd) ENROLLMENTS IN METROPOLITAN AND MICROPOLITAN STATISTICAL AREAS WITH MORE THAN 1,000 INTERNATIONAL STUDENTS, 2004/05

Rank	Metropolitan/Micropolitan Statistical Area * **	Int'l Students
91	Morgantown, WV	1,312
92	Athens-Clarke County, GA	1,311
93	Columbia, SC	1,295
94	Tulsa, OK	1,270
95	Birmingham-Hoover, AL	1,261
96	Indianapolis, IN	1,259
97	Richmond, VA	1,187
98	Fayetteville-Springdale-Rogers, AR-MO	1,183
99	Dayton, OH	1,179
100	Lubbock, TX	1,154
101	Boulder, CO	1,147
102	Charlotte-Gastonia-Concord, NC-SC	1,104
103	St. Cloud, MN	1,079
104	Knoxville, TN	1,064
105	Manhattan, KS Micropolitan Statistical Area	1,037
106	Louisville, KY-IN	1,028
107	Albuquerque, NM	1,010

* "Metropolitan Statistical Area," unless otherwise noted as "Micropolitan Statistical Area."

** Due to some of the changes made by OMB in 2003 in county compositions for many Metropolitan Statistical Areas, as well as the creation of Micropolitan Statistical Areas, comparisons with all but *Open Doors 2004* are not feasible.

3 (cont'd) ENROLLMENTS IN METROPOLITAN AND MICROPOLITAN STATISTICAL AREAS WITH MORE THAN 1,000 INTERNATIONAL STUDENTS, 2004/05

State/Region	1969/70	1979/80	1989/90	1999/00	2000/01	2001/02	2002/03	2003/04	2004/05	% Change from 2003/04
Alaska	73	185	364	392	518	479	393	427	439	2.8
California	22,170	47,621	54,178	66,305	74,281	78,741	80,487	77,186	75,032	-2.8
Hawaii	1,927	2,653	4,190	5,430	5,344	5,289	5,437	5,371	5,485	2.1
Oregon	2,312	4,853	6,403	6,404	6,612	6,560	6,436	5,855	5,490	-6.2
Washington	3,238	6,717	6,858	10,965	11,370	11,624	11,430	10,756	10,674	-0.8
Pacific Total	**29,720**	**62,029**	**71,993**	**89,496**	**98,125**	**102,693**	**104,183**	**99,595**	**97,120**	**-2.5**
Colorado	1,460	4,184	4,681	6,461	6,442	6,692	6,295	5,943	5,496	-7.5
Idaho	500	989	1,150	1,271	1,448	1,578	1,727	1,727	1,923	11.3
Montana	324	401	770	1,011	998	944	871	872	966	10.8
Nevada	109	521	783	2,450	2,755	2,927	2,702	2,743	2,846	3.8
Utah	1,915	3,493	4,862	5,834	6,077	5,950	6,022	5,781	5,918	2.4
Wyoming	282	435	527	487	446	448	491	493	530	7.5
Mountain Total	**4,590**	**10,023**	**12,773**	**17,514**	**18,166**	**18,539**	**18,108**	**17,559**	**17,679**	**0.7**
Illinois	7,795	12,218	16,816	22,807	24,229	25,498	27,116	25,609	25,021	-2.3
Indiana	3,230	5,499	7,575	11,654	12,019	12,871	13,529	13,586	13,149	-3.2
Iowa	1,285	4,010	6,735	7,218	7,840	7,896	7,815	7,699	7,675	-0.3
Kansas	2,005	4,479	6,009	6,050	6,533	7,240	7,000	6,573	6,217	-5.4
Michigan	6,774	10,559	13,555	19,151	21,120	23,103	22,873	22,277	20,879	-6.3
Minnesota	2,577	4,142	5,446	7,888	8,473	8,651	8,985	9,142	8,491	-7.1
Missouri	2,896	4,712	6,620	9,182	10,042	10,281	10,181	9,973	9,540	-4.3
Nebraska	601	1,517	1,918	3,317	3,223	3,874	3,689	3,524	3,915	11.1
North Dakota	616	512	1,341	991	1,126	1,376	1,485	1,595	1,641	2.9
Ohio	4,121	8,672	13,856	16,806	18,502	19,384	18,668	18,770	17,952	-4.4
South Dakota	262	486	758	700	745	770	774	739	665	-10.0
Wisconsin	3,450	4,088	6,438	7,833	7,749	7,701	8,058	7,142	7,798	9.2
Midwest Total	**35,612**	**60,894**	**87,067**	**113,597**	**121,601**	**128,645**	**130,173**	**126,629**	**122,943**	**-2.9**
Alabama	551	3,220	4,513	5,441	5,600	6,040	6,384	6,386	6,359	-0.4
Arkansas	235	1,328	1,710	2,317	2,649	2,758	2,679	2,781	2,784	0.1
Delaware	311	447	1,003	2,016	2,091	1,975	2,230	2,142	2,317	8.2
District of Columbia	3,949	8,499	9,487	8,202	9,094	9,241	8,892	8,532	7,763	-9.0
Florida	6,939	11,919	20,364	24,827	25,366	28,303	27,270	25,861	26,264	1.6
Georgia	1,258	4,472	5,980	9,901	10,844	11,991	12,267	12,010	12,111	0.8
Kentucky	734	2,208	2,543	4,201	4,778	4,789	5,018	4,751	4,792	0.9
Louisiana	1,720	5,546	5,535	6,305	6,400	6,312	6,533	6,621	6,744	1.9
Maryland	1,670	4,266	6,952	11,941	12,409	13,947	12,749	12,633	13,439	6.4
Mississippi	387	1,704	1,941	2,263	2,331	2,381	2,143	2,280	2,266	-0.6
North Carolina	1,594	3,709	5,764	7,848	7,957	8,960	8,599	8,826	9,029	2.3
South Carolina	368	1,484	2,381	3,523	3,573	3,731	3,977	3,919	3,559	-9.2
Tennessee	1,295	4,499	4,247	5,244	5,835	5,867	5,687	5,846	5,767	-1.4
Virginia	662	3,374	6,970	11,616	12,782	12,600	12,875	12,531	12,501	-0.2
West Virginia	226	1,453	1,417	2,230	2,032	2,108	2,173	2,507	2,567	2.4
South Total	**21,899**	**58,128**	**80,807**	**107,875**	**113,741**	**121,003**	**119,476**	**117,626**	**118,262**	**0.5**

4   INTERNATIONAL STUDENTS IN U.S. STATES AND REGIONS, SELECTED YEARS 1969/70 – 2004/05

State/Region	1969/70	1979/80	1989/90	1999/00	2000/01	2001/02	2002/03	2003/04	2004/05	% Change from 2003/04
Arizona	1,134	3,798	6,763	9,405	9,912	10,511	10,325	9,907	10,011	1.0
New Mexico	481	1,240	1,399	1,672	1,629	1,893	1,978	2,111	2,151	1.9
Oklahoma	1,554	8,464	5,989	8,041	8,263	8,818	9,026	8,764	8,454	-3.5
Texas	4,902	24,416	24,170	35,860	37,735	44,192	45,672	45,150	47,367	4.9
Southwest Total	**8,071**	**37,918**	**38,321**	**54,978**	**57,539**	**65,414**	**67,001**	**65,932**	**67,983**	**3.1**
Connecticut	1,314	2,847	4,636	7,110	7,358	8,050	6,603	7,655	7,138	-6.8
Maine	262	307	902	1,282	1,256	1,357	1,383	1,730	1,530	-11.6
Massachusetts	6,352	12,607	20,840	28,192	29,395	29,988	30,039	28,634	27,985	-2.3
New Hampshire	356	501	1,262	2,068	2,301	2,436	2,359	2,128	2,061	-3.1
New Jersey	1,738	4,767	9,608	12,179	12,558	13,516	13,644	13,163	12,571	-4.5
New York	17,701	23,509	38,350	55,085	58,286	62,053	63,773	63,313	61,944	-2.2
Pennsylvania	5,248	8,919	15,803	20,336	22,279	24,014	24,470	23,428	22,773	-2.8
Rhode Island	635	949	1,858	3,176	3,375	3,370	3,193	3,337	3,043	-8.8
Vermont	222	702	1,206	959	949	908	903	835	864	3.5
Northeast Total	**33,828**	**55,108**	**94,465**	**130,387**	**137,757**	**145,692**	**146,367**	**144,223**	**139,909**	**-3.0**
Guam	113	589	473	106	161	162	161	69	63	-8.7
Puerto Rico	1,049	628	633	621	672	743	853	876	976	11.4
Virgin Islands	104	130	319	149	105	105	0*	0	104	-
Other Total	**1,266**	**1,347**	**1,425**	**876**	**938**	**1,010**	**1,014**	**945**	**1,143**	**21.0**
U.S. TOTAL	**134,959**	**286,343**	**386,851**	**514,723**	**547,867**	**582,996**	**586,323**	**572,509**	**565,039**	**-1.3**

* Did not report

4 (cont'd) INTERNATIONAL STUDENTS IN U.S. STATES AND REGIONS, SELECTED YEARS 1969/70 – 2004/05

Primary Source of Funds	2003/04 Int'l Students	2003/04 % of Total	2004/05 Int'l Students	2004/05 % of Total	% Change
Personal & Family	385,543	67.3	349,373	61.8	-9.4
U.S. College or University	134,015	23.4	138,515	24.5	3.4
Home Government/University	13,699	2.4	15,069	2.7	10.0
U.S. Government	2,921	0.5	3,361	0.6	15.1
U.S. Private Sponsor	12,326	2.2	27,094	4.8	119.8
Foreign Private Sponsor	11,888	2.1	6,796	1.2	-42.8
International Organization	1,964	0.3	1,527	0.3	-22.3
Current Employment	10,111	1.8	21,034	3.7	108.0
Other Sources	42	0.0	2,270	0.4	5,304.8
Total	**572,509**	**100.0**	**565,039**	**100.0**	**-1.3**

5 INTERNATIONAL STUDENTS BY PRIMARY SOURCE OF FUNDS, 2003/04 & 2004/05

Primary Source of Funds	% Under-graduate	% Graduate	% Other
Personal & Family	80.9	44.0	54.7
U.S. College or University	9.4	43.6	8.4
Home Government/University	2.4	2.9	2.6
U.S. Government	0.5	0.7	0.3
U.S. Private Sponsor	4.6	5.5	3.1
Foreign Private Sponsor	1.4	1.1	0.6
International Organization	0.2	0.3	0.3
Current Employment	0.3	1.3	29.6
Other Sources	0.2	0.6	0.4
Total	**100.0**	**100.0**	**100.0**

6   PRIMARY SOURCE OF FUNDS WITHIN ACADEMIC LEVEL, 2004/05

Carnegie Category	1999/00	2000/01	2001/02	2002/03	2003/04	2004/05	% Change from 2003/04	% Changes 1999-2005
TOTAL CENSUS	**514,723**	**547,867**	**582,996**	**586,323**	**572,509**	**565,039**	**-1.3**	**9.8**
Doctoral/Research Extensive	258,116	273,974	291,137	296,269	293,072	272,251	-7.1	5.5
Doctoral/Research Intensive	54,861	57,478	62,301	62,672	61,767	59,720	-3.3	8.9
All Doctoral/Research	**312,977**	**331,452**	**353,438**	**358,941**	**354,839**	**331,971**	**-6.4**	**6.1**
Master's I	80,015	86,299	91,749	90,999	88,791	90,929	2.4	13.6
Master's II	4,739	5,523	5,380	4,621	4,896	6,430	31.3	35.7
All Master's	**84,754**	**91,822**	**97,129**	**95,620**	**93,687**	**97,359**	**3.9**	**14.9**
Baccalaureate – Liberal Arts	10,245	9,864	11,046	11,028	11,139	11,775	5.7	14.9
Baccalaureate – General	10,122	10,186	10,719	11,370	11,555	12,334	6.7	21.9
Baccalaureate/Associate's	2,525	2,770	2,671	2,749	2,682	2,615	-2.5	3.6
All Baccalaureate	**22,892**	**22,820**	**24,436**	**25,147**	**25,376**	**26,724**	**5.3**	**16.7**
Associate's	**70,616**	**76,834**	**82,932**	**82,123**	**75,830**	**84,376**	**11.3**	**19.5**
Religious	2,875	2,856	2,888	3,081	3,027	3,764	24.3	30.9
Medical	1,714	1,781	1,934	2,182	2,271	2,682	18.1	56.5
Other Health	2,456	3,088	3,385	2,331	2,377	2,802	17.9	14.1
Engineering	1,962	2,188	2,353	2,292	2,093	2,315	10.6	18.0
Business	4,823	5,103	4,964	4,923	3,755	3,598	-4.2	-25.4
Fine Arts	8,417	8,602	8,308	8,318	7,973	8,333	4.5	-1.0
Law	243	278	243	240	239	316	32.2	30.0
Teachers	114	113	94	95	51	89	74.5	-21.9
Other Specialized	880	928	890	1,029	990	705	-28.8	-19.9
Tribal Colleges	0	2	2	1	1	5	400.0	-
All Specialized	**23,484**	**24,939**	**25,061**	**24,492**	**22,777**	**24,609**	**8.0**	**4.8**

7   INTERNATIONAL STUDENT ENROLLMENTS BY INSTITUTIONAL TYPE, 1999/00 – 2004/05

RANK	DOCTORAL/RESEARCH EXTENSIVE/INTENSIVE		MASTER'S I&II		BACCALAUREATE I & II, BACCALAUREATE/ASSOCIATE'S		ASSOCIATE'S		OTHER INSTITUTIONS	
	Place of Origin	% of Enrollment	Place of Origin	% of Enrollment	Place of Origin	% of Enrollment	Place of Origin	% of Enrollment	Place of Origin	% of Enrollment
1	India	17.7	India	12.1	Canada	11.1	Japan	15.0	Japan	20.5
2	China	14.7	Japan	11.1	Japan	9.6	Korea, Republic of	9.5	Canada	14.1
3	Korea, Republic of	10.2	Korea, Republic of	6.1	Korea, Republic of	7.1	Mexico	4.3	Korea, Republic of	13.3
4	Taiwan	4.7	Taiwan	5.7	India	4.9	Taiwan	3.4	India	6.8
5	Canada	4.5	Canada	5.0	China	2.9	India	3.3	China	5.3
6	Japan	4.5	China	4.8	Bulgaria	2.6	China	3.1	Taiwan	4.4
7	Turkey	2.6	Mexico	2.7	Nepal	2.5	Colombia	3.0	Thailand	1.8
8	Mexico	2.0	Kenya	2.3	United Kingdom	2.3	Hong Kong	2.6	Germany	1.3
9	Germany	1.6	Thailand	2.1	Jamaica	2.1	Canada	2.4	Mexico	1.2
10	United Kingdom	1.5	Turkey	1.9	Ghana	2.1	Kenya	2.4	Turkey	1.2
11	Thailand	1.5	Nepal	1.9	Kenya	2.0	Indonesia	2.1	Colombia	1.2
12	France	1.3	Indonesia	1.7	Taiwan	1.8	Brazil	2.0	Kenya	1.1
13	Malaysia	1.3	Germany	1.7	Nigeria	1.7	Venezuela	1.8	United Kingdom	1.1
14	Indonesia	1.2	Nigeria	1.6	Germany	1.6	Vietnam	1.7	Indonesia	1.0
15	Brazil	1.1	United Kingdom	1.5	Trinidad & Tobago	1.6	Philippines	1.7	Brazil	1.0
16	Hong Kong	1.1	Pakistan	1.4	Pakistan	1.5	Jamaica	1.6	Venezuela	1.0
17	Colombia	1.1	Brazil	1.3	Brazil	1.5	Peru	1.5	Israel	0.9
18	Pakistan	1.0	Colombia	1.2	Mexico	1.5	Nepal	1.5	France	0.7
19	Nigeria	1.0	Hong Kong	1.1	Turkey	1.4	Pakistan	1.5	Nigeria	0.6
20	Russia	0.9	Sweden	1.1	Hong Kong	1.2	Nigeria	1.3	Hong Kong	0.6
TOTAL	250,394		66,412		16,827		51,837		19,002	

8   **TOP 20 PLACES OF ORIGIN OF INTERNATIONAL STUDENTS BY INSTITUTIONAL TYPE, 2004/05**

Rank	Institution	City	State	Total Int'l Students	Total Enrollment
1	University of Southern California	Los Angeles	CA	6,846	30,000
2	University of Illinois at Urbana-Champaign	Champaign	IL	5,560	40,360
3	University of Texas at Austin	Austin	TX	5,333	50,377
4	Columbia University	New York	NY	5,278	23,775
5	New York University	New York	NY	5,140	38,188
6	Purdue University, Main Campus	West Lafayette	IN	4,921	38,653
7	University of Michigan – Ann Arbor	Ann Arbor	MI	4,632	39,031
8	Boston University	Boston	MA	4,541	29,596
9	University of California – Los Angeles	Los Angeles	CA	4,217	37,563
10	The Ohio State University, Main Campus	Columbus	OH	4,140	50,995
11	SUNY – University at Buffalo	Buffalo	NY	3,965	27,276
12	University of Wisconsin – Madison	Madison	WI	3,941	41,169
13	Texas A&M University	College Station	TX	3,721	44,813
14	University of Pennsylvania	Philadelphia	PA	3,712	23,305
15	University of Maryland College Park	College Park	MD	3,646	34,933
16	Harvard University	Cambridge	MA	3,546	19,731
17	Indiana University at Bloomington	Bloomington	IN	3,525	37,821
18	University of Florida	Gainesville	FL	3,492	48,876
19	University of Houston	Houston	TX	3,326	34,912
20	Michigan State University	East Lansing	MI	3,315	44,452
21	University of Minnesota – Twin Cities	Minneapolis	MN	3,302	50,594
22	Penn State University – University Park	University Park	PA	3,237	41,795
23	Florida International University	Miami	FL	3,155	34,876
24	Cornell University	Ithaca	NY	3,119	19,518
25	University of Arizona	Tucson	AZ	3,106	36,932
26	Stanford University	Stanford	CA	3,102	14,846
27	Wayne State University	Detroit	MI	3,066	33,091
28	Arizona State University – Tempe Campus	Tempe	AZ	2,779	49,171
29	University of Texas at Arlington	Arlington	TX	2,732	24,979
30	Massachusetts Institute of Technology	Cambridge	MA	2,723	10,340
31	University of California – Berkeley	Berkeley	CA	2,700	32,814
32	Rutgers, The State U. of NJ – New Brunswick	New Brunswick	NJ	2,647	35,318
33	The University of Texas at Dallas	Richardson	TX	2,625	14,092
34	Georgia Institute of Technology	Atlanta	GA	2,568	16,841
35	University of Washington	Seattle	WA	2,560	39,199
36	Carnegie Mellon University	Pittsburgh	PA	2,559	9,803
37	University of Chicago	Chicago	IL	2,517	13,400
38	University of Iowa	Iowa City	IA	2,373	29,745
39	Iowa State University	Ames	IA	2,295	26,380
40	Johns Hopkins University	Baltimore	MD	2,292	18,659

9   INTERNATIONAL STUDENTS BY INSTITUTIONAL TYPE: TOP 40 DOCTORAL/RESEARCH INSTITUTIONS, 2004/05

Rank	Institution	City	State	Total Int'l Students	Total Enrollment
1	San Francisco State University	San Francisco	CA	2,175	29,686
2	San Jose State University	San Jose	CA	1,529	28,932
3	California State University – Fullerton	Fullerton	CA	1,464	32,744
4	Hawaii Pacific University	Honolulu	HI	1,429	7,900
5	Rochester Institute of Technology	Rochester	NY	1,346	15,338
6	California State University – Northridge	Northridge	CA	1,343	31,074
7	California State University – East Bay	Hayward	CA	1,341	13,237
8	California State University – Long Beach	Long Beach	CA	1,315	33,479
9	University of Central Oklahoma	Edmond	OK	1,220	15,246
10	CUNY Baruch College	New York	NY	1,205	15,700
11	NY Institute of Technology – Old Westbury	Old Westbury	NY	1,166	10,646
12	CUNY The City College of New York	New York	NY	1,126	12,543
13	CUNY Hunter College	New York	NY	1,077	20,845
13	Strayer University	Washington	DC	1,077	20,138
15	Fairleigh Dickinson U. – Florham & Metropolitan	Teaneck	NJ	1,028	11,381
16	Johnson & Wales University	Providence	RI	980	15,130
17	Eastern Michigan University	Ypsilanti	MI	970	23,862
18	California State University – Los Angeles	Los Angeles	CA	935	20,637
19	St. Cloud State University	St. Cloud	MN	924	15,608
20	University of Texas at San Antonio	San Antonio	TX	897	24,665
21	CUNY Brooklyn College	Brooklyn	NY	864	15,513
22	University of Nebraska at Omaha	Omaha	NE	826	14,959
23	University of North Carolina at Charlotte	Charlotte	NC	818	20,000
24	California State Polytechnic University – Pomona	Pomona	CA	774	19,804
25	Montclair State University	Upper Montclair	NJ	745	15,637
26	California State University – Fresno	Fresno	CA	716	17,521
27	Towson University	Towson	MD	650	17,667
28	University of Texas – Pan American	Edinburg	TX	645	17,030
29	Santa Clara University	Santa Clara	CA	633	7,082
30	California State University – Sacramento	Sacramento	CA	631	27,972
31	California State University – San Bernardino	San Bernardino	CA	619	17,000
32	Suffolk University	Boston	MA	616	6,660
33	Oklahoma City University	Oklahoma City	OK	615	3,668
34	University of Maryland University College	Adelphi	MD	612	28,374
35	Minnesota State University, Mankato	Mankato	MN	581	14,153
36	Lamar University	Beaumont	TX	573	10,804
37	University of Houston – Clear Lake	Houston	TX	564	7,785
38	Western Kentucky University	Bowling Green	KY	558	18,500
39	CUNY Queens College	Flushing	NY	553	16,993
40	University of the District of Columbia	Washington	DC	544	5,424

10   INTERNATIONAL STUDENTS BY INSTITUTIONAL TYPE: TOP 40 MASTER'S INSTITUTIONS, 2004/05

Rank	Institution	City	State	Total Int'l Students	Total Enrollment
1	Brigham Young University – Hawaii Campus	Laie	HI	1,117	2,846
2	SUNY – Fashion Institute of Technology	New York	NY	1,087	6,668
3	Utah Valley State College	Orem	UT	454	24,149
4	University of Dallas	Irving	TX	423	3,159
5	University of Hawaii at Hilo	Hilo	HI	371	3,337
6	Mount Holyoke College	South Hadley	MA	350	2,100
7	Calvin College	Grand Rapids	MI	324	4,180
8	University of Maine at Fort Kent	Fort Kent	ME	298	1,076
9	Daemen College	Amherst	NY	292	2,186
10	CUNY New York City College of Technology	Brooklyn	NY	275	11,700
11	Wesleyan University	Middletown	CT	266	3,221
12	Macalester College	St. Paul	MN	262	1,865
13	St. Francis College	Brooklyn Heights	NY	260	2,326
14	Smith College	Northampton	MA	239	3,089
15	Middlebury College	Middlebury	VT	205	2,357
16	Wellesley College	Wellesley	MA	204	2,289
17	Oberlin College	Oberlin	OH	188	2,827
18	Ramapo College of New Jersey	Mahwah	NJ	186	5,617
19	Lakeland College	Sheboygan	WI	182	4,019
19	Ohio Wesleyan University	Delaware	OH	182	1,944
21	Grinnell College	Grinnell	IA	180	1,485
22	Colgate University	Hamilton	NY	170	2,720
23	Drew University	Madison	NJ	169	2,675
24	Southwest Minnesota State University	Marshall	MN	164	3,189
25	Lee University	Cleveland	TN	162	3,806
26	CUNY York College	Jamaica	NY	161	6,250
27	CUNY Medgar Evers College	Brooklyn	NY	159	5,000
28	Franklin & Marshall College	Lancaster	PA	158	1,993
29	Mercyhurst College	Erie	PA	152	3,795
30	Graceland University	Lamoni	IA	150	2,351
31	College of Saint Benedict/Saint John's University	Collegeville	MN	147	4,048
32	Lawrence University	Appleton	WI	146	1,390
33	Coastal Carolina University	Conway	SC	144	7,021
33	Dordt College	Sioux Center	IA	144	1,285
35	Metropolitan State College of Denver	Denver	CO	143	20,230
36	Bethune Cookman College	Daytona Beach	FL	137	2,838
36	Colby College	Waterville	ME	137	1,821
38	Concordia College – Moorhead	Moorhead	MN	136	2,814
39	Eckerd College	St. Petersburg	FL	129	1,631
40	Vassar College	Poughkeepsie	NY	127	2,475
40	Willamette University	Salem	OR	127	2,663

11   **INTERNATIONAL STUDENTS BY INSTITUTIONAL TYPE: TOP 40 BACCALAUREATE INSTITUTIONS, 2004/05**

Rank	Institution	City	State	Total Int'l Students	Total Enrollment
1	Houston Community College	Houston	TX	3,702	37,846
2	Santa Monica College	Santa Monica	CA	2,557	25,495
3	Montgomery College	Rockville	MD	2,100	22,254
4	De Anza College	Cupertino	CA	2,083	23,277
5	CUNY Borough of Manhattan Community College	New York	NY	1,660	18,854
6	Miami-Dade Community College	Miami	FL	1,490	58,490
7	North Harris Montgomery Community College District	The Woodlands	TX	1,414	35,479
8	City College of San Francisco	San Francisco	CA	1,322	37,166
9	Nassau Community College	Garden City	NY	1,235	20,984
10	Foothill College	Los Altos Hills	CA	1,209	16,256
11	Seminole Community College	Sanford	FL	1,132	17,495
12	CUNY Queensborough Community College	Bayside	NY	1,117	12,470
13	Pasadena City College	Pasadena	CA	977	25,564
14	Richland College	Dallas	TX	892	14,100
15	Phoenix College	Phoenix	AZ	858	12,440
16	North Lake College	Irving	TX	834	8,664
17	Collin County Community College District	Plano	TX	804	17,702
18	El Camino College	Torrance	CA	800	25,000
19	CUNY La Guardia Community College	Long Island City	NY	796	12,768
20	Austin Community College	Austin	TX	792	35,662
21	Oakland Community College	Waterford	MI	769	26,012
22	Diablo Valley College	Pleasant Hill	CA	728	17,638
23	Los Angeles City College	Los Angeles	CA	725	14,854
24	Community College of Southern Nevada	Las Vegas	NV	692	34,000
25	Broward Community College	Fort Lauderdale	FL	680	37,358
26	Orange Coast College	Costa Mesa	CA	652	25,595
27	Georgia Perimeter College	Clarkston	GA	625	18,986
28	CUNY Kingsborough Community College	Brooklyn	NY	612	15,356
29	Grossmont College	El Cajon	CA	598	16,544
29	Seattle Central Community College	Seattle	WA	598	9,853
31	Bellevue Community College	Bellevue	WA	594	19,142
32	Edmonds Community College	Lynnwood	WA	593	10,924
33	Glendale Community College	Glendale	CA	574	15,700
34	Bergen Community College	Paramus	NJ	548	13,506
35	Santa Barbara City College	Santa Barbara	CA	527	16,533
36	Peralta Community College District	Oakland	CA	522	25,174
37	Bunker Hill Community College	Boston	MA	515	7,412
38	Prince George's Community College	Largo	MD	510	31,857
39	Quincy College	Quincy	MA	507	4,538
40	Shoreline Community College	Seattle	WA	506	8,250

12 INTERNATIONAL STUDENTS BY INSTITUTIONAL TYPE: TOP 40 ASSOCIATE'S INSTITUTIONS, 2004/05

Rank	Institution	City	State	Total Int'l Students	Total Enrollment
1	Academy of Art University	San Francisco	CA	1,777	7,000
2	D'Youville College	Buffalo	NY	1,495	2,700
3	Berklee College of Music	Boston	MA	916	4,963
4	Pratt Institute	Brooklyn	NY	684	3,801
5	Southern Polytechnic State University	Marietta	GA	626	3,267
6	School of Visual Arts	New York	NY	597	5,952
7	Southern New Hampshire University	Manchester	NH	579	3,288
8	Babson College	Babson Park	MA	573	4,096
9	Golden Gate University	San Francisco	CA	571	6,776
10	Savannah College of Art and Design	Savannah	GA	550	2,728
11	School of the Art Institute of Chicago	Chicago	IL	401	6,823
12	Franklin University	Columbus	OH	394	6,414
13	Fuller Theological Seminary	Pasadena	CA	388	3,325
14	University of Texas Health Science Ctr. at Houston	Houston	TX	352	2,887
15	Southwestern Baptist Theological Seminary	Fort Worth	TX	346	2,887
16	The Art Institute of Fort Lauderdale	Fort Lauderdale	FL	313	800
17	Manhattan School of Music	New York	NY	300	790
18	Colorado School of Mines	Golden	CO	297	2,604
19	Rhode Island School of Design	Providence	RI	268	3,983
20	Arizona State University East	Mesa	AZ	217	2,004
21	Tufts U. - Fletcher School of Law & Diplomacy	Medford	MA	215	5,030
22	University of Medicine & Dentistry of New Jersey	Newark	NJ	203	1,290
23	Baylor College of Medicine	Houston	TX	187	1,290
24	Northwestern Polytechnic University	Fremont	CA	186	412
25	Bethesda Christian University	Anaheim	CA	182	1,795
26	U. of Texas, Southwestern Medical Center at Dallas	Dallas	TX	175	1,713
27	Asbury Theological Seminary	Wilmore	KY	172	1,400
28	Miami International University of Art & Design	Miami	FL	167	1,220
29	Life University - College of Chiropractic	Marietta	GA	161	1,182
30	American InterContinental University	Atlanta	GA	155	1,600
30	Palmer College of Chiropractic	Davenport	IA	155	1,860
32	Davenport University	Grand Rapids	MI	147	13,531
32	Oregon Health & Science University	Portland	OR	147	2,553
34	Louisiana State University - Health Sciences Center	New Orleans	LA	142	2,837
35	Southern Baptist Theological Seminary	Louisville	KY	135	2,811
36	University of Texas Health Science Ctr. at San Antonio	San Antonio	TX	125	1,043
37	Otis College of Art & Design	Los Angeles	CA	122	1,050
38	Calvin Theological Seminary	Grand Rapids	MI	121	290
38	U. of Oklahoma Health Sciences Center	Oklahoma City	OK	121	2,121
40	University of Texas Medical Branch Galveston	Galveston	TX	117	2,345

13   **INTERNATIONAL STUDENTS BY INSTITUTIONAL TYPE: TOP 40 SPECIALIZED INSTITUTIONS, 2004/05**

Rank	Institution	City	State	Total Int'l Students	Total Enrollment
1	University of Southern California	Los Angeles	CA	6,846	30,000
2	University of Illinois at Urbana-Champaign	Champaign	IL	5,560	40,360
3	University of Texas at Austin	Austin	TX	5,333	50,377
4	Columbia University	New York	NY	5,278	23,775
5	New York University	New York	NY	5,140	38,188
6	Purdue University, Main Campus	West Lafayette	IN	4,921	38,653
7	University of Michigan – Ann Arbor	Ann Arbor	MI	4,632	39,031
8	Boston University	Boston	MA	4,541	29,596
9	University of California – Los Angeles	Los Angeles	CA	4,217	37,563
10	The Ohio State University, Main Campus	Columbus	OH	4,140	50,995
11	SUNY – University at Buffalo	Buffalo	NY	3,965	27,276
12	University of Wisconsin – Madison	Madison	WI	3,941	41,169
13	Texas A&M University	College Station	TX	3,721	44,813
14	University of Pennsylvania	Philadelphia	PA	3,712	23,305
15	Houston Community College	Houston	TX	3,702	37,846
16	University of Maryland College Park	College Park	MD	3,646	34,933
17	Harvard University	Cambridge	MA	3,546	19,731
18	Indiana University at Bloomington	Bloomington	IN	3,525	37,821
19	University of Florida	Gainesville	FL	3,492	48,876
20	University of Houston	Houston	TX	3,326	34,912
21	Michigan State University	East Lansing	MI	3,315	44,452
22	University of Minnesota – Twin Cities	Minneapolis	MN	3,302	50,594
23	Penn State University – University Park	University Park	PA	3,237	41,795
24	Florida International University	Miami	FL	3,155	34,876
25	Cornell University	Ithaca	NY	3,119	19,518
26	University of Arizona	Tucson	AZ	3,106	36,932
27	Stanford University	Stanford	CA	3,102	14,846
28	Wayne State University	Detroit	MI	3,066	33,091
29	Arizona State University – Tempe Campus	Tempe	AZ	2,779	49,171
30	University of Texas at Arlington	Arlington	TX	2,732	24,979
31	Massachusetts Institute of Technology	Cambridge	MA	2,723	10,340
32	University of California – Berkeley	Berkeley	CA	2,700	32,814
33	Rutgers, The State U. of NJ – New Brunswick	New Brunswick	NJ	2,647	35,318
34	The University of Texas at Dallas	Richardson	TX	2,625	14,092
35	Georgia Institute of Technology	Atlanta	GA	2,568	16,841
36	University of Washington	Seattle	WA	2,560	39,199
37	Carnegie Mellon University	Pittsburgh	PA	2,559	9,803
38	Santa Monica College	Santa Monica	CA	2,557	25,495
39	University of Chicago	Chicago	IL	2,517	13,400
40	University of Iowa	Iowa City	IA	2,373	29,745
41	Iowa State University	Ames	IA	2,295	26,380
42	Johns Hopkins University	Baltimore	MD	2,292	18,659
43	Brigham Young University	Provo	UT	2,253	33,328
44	Syracuse University	Syracuse	NY	2,200	18,247
45	University of Texas at El Paso	El Paso	TX	2,187	18,918

14 **INSTITUTIONS WITH 1,000 OR MORE INTERNATIONAL STUDENTS:
RANKED BY INTERNATIONAL STUDENT TOTAL, 2004/05**

Rank	Institution	City	State	Total Int'l Students	Total Enrollment
46	San Francisco State University	San Francisco	CA	2,175	29,686
47	SUNY – Stony Brook University	Stony Brook	NY	2,146	22,344
48	Northeastern University	Boston	MA	2,104	23,556
49	Northwestern University	Evanston	IL	2,102	17,762
49	Virginia Polytechnic Institute & State University	Blacksburg	VA	2,102	27,619
51	Montgomery College	Rockville	MD	2,100	22,254
52	De Anza College	Cupertino	CA	2,083	23,277
53	University of Illinois at Chicago	Chicago	IL	2,049	25,763
54	Illinois Institute of Technology	Chicago	IL	2,032	6,378
55	University of South Florida	Tampa	FL	2,006	42,133
56	Oklahoma State University, Main Campus	Stillwater	OK	1,999	23,571
57	Temple University	Philadelphia	PA	1,963	33,286
58	University of Cincinnati	Cincinnati	OH	1,943	27,601
59	University of California – San Diego	La Jolla	CA	1,928	25,278
60	George Washington University	Washington	DC	1,887	24,092
61	University of California – Irvine	Irvine	CA	1,875	24,919
62	University of North Texas	Denton	TX	1,861	32,399
63	Duke University & Medical Center	Durham	NC	1,860	13,622
64	Louisiana State University	Baton Rouge	LA	1,815	31,561
65	University of Connecticut	Storrs	CT	1,800	26,629
66	University of California – Davis	Davis	CA	1,794	30,065
67	Academy of Art University	San Francisco	CA	1,777	7,000
68	Yale University	New Haven	CT	1,759	11,359
69	The New School	New York	NY	1,755	8,812
70	University of Virginia, Main Campus	Charlottesville	VA	1,743	21,000
71	University of Massachusetts at Amherst	Amherst	MA	1,724	24,310
72	University of Hawaii at Manoa	Honolulu	HI	1,703	20,549
73	University of Utah	Salt Lake City	UT	1,701	28,933
74	Georgia State University	Atlanta	GA	1,700	27,267
75	Drexel University	Philadelphia	PA	1,670	17,000
76	University of Pittsburgh, Main Campus	Pittsburgh	PA	1,667	26,731
77	CUNY Borough of Manhattan Community College	New York	NY	1,660	18,854
78	Georgetown University	Washington	DC	1,645	13,233
79	University of Oklahoma – Norman	Norman	OK	1,644	25,053
80	University of Delaware	Newark	DE	1,642	21,121
81	University of Kansas	Lawrence	KS	1,617	29,272
82	University of Miami	Coral Gables	FL	1,593	15,133
83	Washington University in St. Louis	St. Louis	MO	1,582	13,020
84	North Carolina State University	Raleigh	NC	1,581	29,854
85	University of Missouri – Columbia	Columbia	MO	1,562	27,003
86	Washington State University	Pullman	WA	1,545	23,324
87	Southern Illinois University Carbondale	Carbondale	IL	1,542	21,387
88	George Mason University	Fairfax	VA	1,537	28,874
89	San Jose State University	San Jose	CA	1,529	28,932
90	Florida State University	Tallahassee	FL	1,507	38,516

14 (cont'd) INSTITUTIONS WITH 1,000 OR MORE INTERNATIONAL STUDENTS: RANKED BY INTERNATIONAL STUDENT TOTAL, 2004/05

Rank	Institution	City	State	Total Int'l Students	Total Enrollment
91	University of North Carolina at Chapel Hill	Chapel Hill	NC	1,497	26,359
92	D'Youville College	Buffalo	NY	1,495	2,700
93	University of Oregon	Eugene	OR	1,493	20,339
94	Miami-Dade Community College	Miami	FL	1,490	58,490
95	Florida Atlantic University	Boca Raton	FL	1,473	25,383
96	Western Michigan University	Kalamazoo	MI	1,467	27,829
97	California State University – Fullerton	Fullerton	CA	1,464	32,744
98	San Diego State University	San Diego	CA	1,460	32,936
99	University of Kentucky	Lexington	KY	1,457	26,260
100	Hawaii Pacific University	Honolulu	HI	1,429	7,900
101	New Jersey Institute of Technology	Newark	NJ	1,414	8,249
101	North Harris Montgomery Community College District	The Woodlands	TX	1,414	35,479
103	University of Nebraska – Lincoln	Lincoln	NE	1,390	22,559
104	University of Central Florida	Orlando	FL	1,354	42,847
105	Rochester Institute of Technology	Rochester	NY	1,346	15,338
106	California State University – Northridge	Northridge	CA	1,343	31,074
107	California State University – East Bay	Hayward	CA	1,341	13,237
108	City College of San Francisco	San Francisco	CA	1,322	37,166
109	California State University – Long Beach	Long Beach	CA	1,315	33,479
110	West Virginia University	Morgantown	WV	1,312	25,255
111	The University of Georgia	Athens	GA	1,311	33,405
112	SUNY – Binghamton University	Binghamton	NY	1,297	13,860
113	Ohio University, Main Campus	Athens	OH	1,293	19,962
114	University of Nevada, Las Vegas	Las Vegas	NV	1,286	27,344
115	Nassau Community College	Garden City	NY	1,235	20,984
116	Wichita State University	Wichita	KS	1,221	14,297
117	University of Central Oklahoma	Edmond	OK	1,220	15,246
118	Foothill College	Los Altos Hills	CA	1,209	16,256
119	Princeton University	Princeton	NJ	1,206	6,708
120	CUNY Baruch College	New York	NY	1,205	15,700
121	Case Western Reserve University	Cleveland	OH	1,175	9,186
122	NY Institute of Technology – Old Westbury	Old Westbury	NY	1,166	10,646
123	University of Bridgeport	Bridgeport	CT	1,164	3,340
124	Texas Tech University	Lubbock	TX	1,141	28,325
125	University of Rochester	Rochester	NY	1,140	7,250
126	Seminole Community College	Sanford	FL	1,132	17,495
127	CUNY The City College of New York	New York	NY	1,126	12,543
128	Brigham Young University – Hawaii	Laie	HI	1,117	2,846
128	CUNY Queensborough Community College	Bayside	NY	1,117	12,470
130	SUNY – Fashion Institute of Technology	New York	NY	1,087	6,668
131	University of Alabama at Birmingham	Birmingham	AL	1,086	16,695
131	University of Colorado at Boulder	Boulder	CO	1,086	29,151
133	Brown University	Providence	RI	1,083	8,121
134	CUNY Hunter College	New York	NY	1,077	20,845
134	Strayer University	Washington	DC	1,077	20,138

14 (cont'd) INSTITUTIONS WITH 1,000 OR MORE INTERNATIONAL STUDENTS: RANKED BY INTERNATIONAL STUDENT TOTAL, 2004/05

Rank	Institution	City	State	Total Int'l Students	Total Enrollment
136	Old Dominion University	Norfolk	VA	1,072	20,802
137	Kansas State University	Manhattan	KS	1,037	22,958
137	Portland State University	Portland	OR	1,037	21,030
139	Emory University	Atlanta	GA	1,031	11,781
140	Fairleigh Dickinson U. – Florham & Metropolitan	Teaneck	NJ	1,028	11,381
141	Howard University	Washington	DC	1,017	10,642
142	Tulane University	New Orleans	LA	1,016	12,000
143	University of California – Riverside	Riverside	CA	1,013	17,296
144	Rensselaer Polytechnic Institute	Troy	NY	1,003	8,265
145	University of California – Santa Barbara	Santa Barbara	CA	1,000	21,026

14 (cont'd) INSTITUTIONS WITH 1,000 OR MORE INTERNATIONAL STUDENTS: RANKED BY INTERNATIONAL STUDENT TOTAL, 2004/05

Field of Study	2003/04 Int'l Students	2004/05 Int'l Students	2004/05 % of Total	% Change
Agriculture, Total	**7,292**	**7,519**	**1.3**	**3.1**
Agriculture, Agriculture Operations, and Related Sciences (1)	5,406	5,528	1.0	2.3
Natural Resources and Conservation	1,886	1,991	0.4	5.6
Business and Management, Total	**108,788**	**100,079**	**17.7**	**-8.0**
Business and Management, General (2)	107,909	98,975	17.5	-8.3
Consumer, Personal, and Miscellaneous Services	879	1,104	0.2	25.6
Education	**15,909**	**15,697**	**2.8**	**-1.3**
Engineering, Total	**95,220**	**92,952**	**16.5**	**-2.4**
Engineering, General	87,528	87,999	15.6	0.5
Engineering-Related Technologies	5,920	3,427	0.6	-42.1
Transportation and Material Moving	1,012	977	0.2	-3.5
Mechanics and Repairers	486	277	0.0	-43.0
Construction Trades	184	242	0.0	31.5
Precision Production	90	30	0.0	-66.7
Fine and Applied Arts, Total	**31,882**	**28,063**	**5.0**	**-12.0**
Visual and Performing Arts	25,204	21,792	3.9	-13.5
Architecture and Environmental Design	6,678	6,271	1.1	-6.1
Health Professions (3)	**25,749**	**26,301**	**4.7**	**2.1**

15 INTERNATIONAL STUDENTS BY FIELD OF STUDY, 2003/04 & 2004/05

Field of Study	2003/04 Int'l Students	2004/05 Int'l Students	2004/05 % of Total	% Change
Humanities, Total	**16,622**	**15,850**	**2.8**	**-4.6**
Letters	4,841	4,590	0.8	-5.2
Foreign Languages	5,366	5,839	1.0	8.8
Theology	4,172	3,877	0.7	-7.1
Philosophy and Religion	2,243	1,544	0.3	-31.2
Mathematics and Computer Sciences, Total	**67,693**	**50,747**	**9.0**	**-25.0**
Computer and Information Sciences	57,739	38,966	6.9	-32.5
Mathematics	9,954	11,781	2.1	18.4
Physical and Life Sciences, Total	**44,607**	**49,499**	**8.8**	**11.0**
Physical Sciences	19,603	22,498	4.0	14.8
Life Sciences	23,290	25,987	4.6	11.6
Science Technologies	1,714	1,014	0.2	-40.8
Social Sciences, Total	**54,153**	**46,085**	**8.2**	**-14.9**
History (3)	-	1,774	0.3	-
Social Sciences, General (4)	34,101	25,075	4.4	-26.5
Psychology	8,352	7,788	1.4	-6.8
Public Administration and Social Service (5)	5,372	5,056	0.9	-5.9
Area and Ethnic Studies	2,639	2,570	0.5	-2.6
Security and Protective Services (6)	817	882	0.2	8.0
Parks and Recreation	2,872	2,940	0.5	2.4
Other, Total	**60,273**	**59,700**	**10.6**	**-1.0**
Liberal/General Studies	32,007	32,912	5.8	2.8
Communications and Journalism	9,104	9,107	1.6	0.0
Law	6,222	6,270	1.1	0.8
Multi/Interdisciplinary Studies	7,057	5,611	1.0	-20.5
Family and Consumer Sciences/Human Sciences (7)	2,801	3,142	0.6	12.2
Library and Archival Sciences	742	638	0.1	-14.0
Communication Technologies	2,335	1,848	0.3	-20.9
Military Technologies	5	18	0.0	260.0
Residency Programs (2)	-	154	0.0	-
Intensive English Language	**15,006**	**16,133**	**2.6**	**7.5**
Undeclared	**29,313**	**27,982**	**5.1**	**-4.5**
Optional Practical Training (OPT) (8)	**-**	**28,432**	**5.0**	**-**
TOTAL	**572,509**	**565,039**	**100.0**	**-1.3**

(1) Formerly "Agricultural Sciences" and "Agribusiness and Agricultural Production"   (2) Includes former "Marketing & Distribution"   (3) New CIP category
(4) Formerly included "History"   (5) Formerly "Public Administration"   (6) Formerly "Protective Services"   (7) Formerly "Home Economics" & includes former
"Vocational Home Economics"   (8) New IIE category

15   (cont'd) INTERNATIONAL STUDENTS BY FIELD OF STUDY, 2003/04 & 2004/05

Doctoral/Research Institutions	% Enrollment		Associate's Institutions	% Enrollment
Engineering	21.6		Other	28.7
Business & Management	14.7		Business & Management	19.5
Other	14.2		Undeclared	16.4
Physical & Life Sciences	10.7		Health Professions	8.7
Mathematics & Computer Sciences	9.3		Mathematics & Computer Sciences	6.5
Social Sciences	9.0		Engineering	5.2
Undeclared	5.7		Fine & Applied Arts	4.8
Fine & Applied Arts	4.0		Social Sciences	3.3
Health Professions	3.8		Physical & Life Sciences	3.1
Humanities	2.6		Education	1.7
Education	2.6		Humanities	1.5
Agriculture	1.8		Agriculture	0.4
Intensive English Language*	0.0		Intensive English Language*	0.0

Master's Institutions	% Enrollment		Specialized Institutions	% Enrollment
Business & Management	30.8		Fine & Applied Arts	33.2
Other	12.8		Health Professions	13.9
Mathematics & Computer Sciences	11.2		Business & Management	11.6
Undeclared	9.6		Humanities	10.6
Social Sciences	8.1		Other	7.8
Engineering	8.1		Physical & Life Sciences	7.6
Physical & Life Sciences	4.9		Engineering	5.5
Education	4.2		Mathematics & Computer Sciences	3.5
Health Professions	3.8		Social Sciences	2.9
Fine & Applied Arts	3.7		Undeclared	1.6
Humanities	2.5		Education	1.6
Agriculture	0.5		Agriculture	0.1
Intensive English Language*	0.0		Intensive English Language*	0.0

Baccalaureate Institutions	% Enrollment
Business & Management	20.3
Other	18.0
Undeclared	16.3
Social Sciences	12.7
Physical & Life Sciences	7.6
Mathematics & Computer Sciences	6.5
Education	5.2
Fine & Applied Arts	4.3
Humanities	3.9
Health Professions	2.5
Engineering	2.1
Agriculture	0.5
Intensive English Language*	0.0

* Less than 0.1% of the total enrollment.

16   FIELDS OF STUDY BY INSTITUTIONAL TYPE, 2004/05

Academic Level	2003/04 Int'l Students	2003/04 % of Total	2004/05 Int'l Students	2004/05 % of Total	% Change
Associate's	**69,541**	**12.1**	**65,667**	**11.6**	**-5.6**
Bachelor's	**178,659**	**31.2**	**173,545**	**30.7**	**-2.9**
Freshman	32,489	5.7	29,780	5.3	-8.3
Sophomore	28,265	4.9	26,351	4.7	-6.8
Junior	36,312	6.3	33,947	6.0	-6.5
Senior	48,281	8.4	45,431	8.0	-5.9
Unspecified	33,312	5.8	38,036	6.7	14.2
Graduate	**274,310**	**47.9**	**264,410**	**46.8**	**-3.6**
Master's	142,271	24.9	121,523	21.5	-14.6
Doctoral	100,092	17.5	102,084	18.1	2.0
Professional Training	8,212	1.4	7,675	1.4	-6.5
Unspecified	23,735	4.1	33,128	5.9	39.6
Other	**49,999**	**8.7**	**61,417**	**10.9**	**22.8**
Practical Training	29,340	5.1	32,999	5.8	12.5
Non-Degree	10,435	1.8	15,522	2.7	48.7
Intensive English Language	10,224	1.8	12,896	2.3	26.1
TOTAL	**572,509**	**100.0**	**565,039**	**100.0**	**-1.3**

17   **INTERNATIONAL STUDENTS BY ACADEMIC LEVEL, 2003/04 & 2004/05**

Year	Undergraduate	Graduate	Other
1954/55	19,101	12,118	3,012
1959/60	25,164	18,910	4,412
1964/65	38,130	35,096	8,774
1969/70	63,296	59,112	12,551
1975/76	95,949	83,395	18,073
1979/80	172,378	94,207	19,758
1984/85	197,741	122,476	21,895
1987/88	176,669	156,366	23,152
1988/89	172,551	165,590	28,209
1989/90	184,527	169,827	32,495
1990/91	189,900	182,130	35,500
1991/92	197,070	191,330	31,190
1992/93	210,080	193,330	35,210
1993/94	213,610	201,030	35,110
1994/95	221,500	191,738	39,396
1995/96	218,620	190,092	45,075
1996/97	218,743	190,244	48,997
1997/98	223,276	207,510	50,494
1998/99	235,802	211,426	43,706
1999/00	237,211	218,219	59,293
2000/01	254,429	238,497	54,941
2001/02	261,079	264,749	57,168
2002/03	260,103	267,876	58,344
2003/04	248,200	274,310	49,999
2004/05	239,212	264,410	61,417

18   **INTERNATIONAL STUDENTS BY ACADEMIC LEVEL,
SELECTED YEARS 1954/55 – 2004/05**

Characteristic	% Under-graduate	% Graduate	% Other	Characteristic	% Under-graduate	% Graduate	% Other
Sex				U.S. Government	0.5	0.7	0.3
Male	51.4	59.9	53.0	U.S. Private Sponsor	4.6	5.5	3.1
Female	48.6	40.1	47.0	Foreign Private Sponsor	1.4	1.1	0.6
				International Organization	0.2	0.3	0.3
Marital Status				Current Employment	0.3	1.3	29.6
Single	95.1	77.5	84.2	Other Sources	0.2	0.6	0.4
Married	4.9	22.5	15.8				
				Field of Study			
Enrollment Status				Agriculture	0.6	2.2	0.1
Full-Time	90.9	88.0	34.5	Business & Management	24.3	14.9	3.1
Part-Time	9.1	12.0	7.1	Education	1.8	4.7	0.3
Optional Practical Training	-	-	58.4	Engineering	11.4	23.8	2.5
				Fine & Applied Arts	7.1	4.0	0.9
Visa Type				Health Professions	4.9	5.0	1.8
F Visa	86.7	87.4	84.1	Humanities	1.9	4.1	0.9
J Visa	3.1	5.5	10.7	Math & Computer Sciences	7.8	11.4	1.9
M Visa	0.2	0.0	0.3	Physical & Life Sciences	5.9	13.3	0.9
Other Visa	10.0	7.0	5.0	Social Sciences	8.5	9.0	1.8
				Other	17.1	6.5	51.1
Primary Source of Funds				Intensive English	0.0	0.0	0.0
Personal & Family	80.9	44.0	54.7	Undeclared	8.7	1.1	34.7
U.S. College or University	9.4	43.6	8.4				
Home Gov't/University	2.4	2.9	2.6	**TOTAL**	**239,212**	**264,410**	**61,417**

19 PERSONAL AND ACADEMIC CHARACTERISTICS OF INTERNATIONAL STUDENTS BY ACADEMIC LEVEL, 2004/05

Year	% Male	% Female	% Single	% F Visa	% J Visa	% Other Visa	% Refugee*	Int'l Students
1976/77	69.2	30.8	73.7	75.0	10.4	7.3	7.3	203,068
1977/78	75.0	25.0	77.4	78.8	9.3	6.9	5.0	235,509
1978/79	74.1	25.9	74.7	80.7	9.8	5.7	3.8	263,938
1979/80	72.4	27.6	78.6	82.0	7.6	6.4	4.0	286,343
1980/81	71.7	28.3	80.1	82.9	6.7	5.6	4.8	311,882
1981/82	71.0	29.0	79.3	84.3	6.8	4.9	4.0	326,299
1982/83	70.9	29.1	80.1	84.0	7.2	5.2	3.6	336,985
1983/84	70.6	29.4	80.1	83.2	8.2	5.2	3.4	338,894
1984/85	69.8	30.2	80.4	83.5	8.4	5.1	3.0	342,113
1985/86	70.7	29.3	80.0	81.5	9.2	5.7	3.6	343,777
1986/87	68.9	31.1	79.7	81.0	11.0	5.2	2.8	349,609
1987/88	67.7	32.3	79.8	79.4	12.1	6.1	2.3	356,187
1988/89	66.5	33.5	80.9	79.0	12.5	6.5	2.0	366,354
1989/90	66.1	33.9	80.1	78.5	12.7	6.4	2.4	386,851
1990/91	64.0	36.0	78.5	80.6	11.0	6.4	2.0	407,529
1991/92	63.7	36.3	80.7	84.6	9.5	6.0	.	419,585
1992/93	63.0	37.0	82.5	85.5	8.5	6.1	.	438,618
1993/94	62.1	37.9	83.1	86.4	7.7	5.9	.	449,749
1994/95	60.9	39.1	83.4	85.8	7.7	6.4	.	452,635
1995/96	58.9	41.1	82.6	84.9	7.7	7.3	.	453,787
1996/97	59.0	41.0	84.4	85.6	6.8	7.6	.	457,984
1997/98	58.1	41.9	83.6	86.8	6.7	6.5	.	481,280
1998/99	58.0	42.0	85.2	87.3	6.3	6.4	.	490,933
1999/00	57.5	42.5	84.2	85.6	5.8	8.6	.	514,723
2000/01	57.1	42.9	84.7	85.8	5.8	8.4	.	547,867
2001/02	57.0	43.0	86.0	86.2	5.1	8.7	.	582,996
2002/03	56.2	43.8	85.0	86.0	4.9	9.1	.	586,323
2003/04	55.8	44.2	85.3	85.7	5.1	9.2	.	572,509
2004/05	55.6	44.4	85.4	86.7	5.1	8.2	.	565,039

* After 1990, IIE ceased to collect data on refugee students.

20   PERSONAL CHARACTERISTICS OF INTERNATIONAL STUDENTS, 1976/77 – 2004/05

IN THIS SECTION

TABLE	SOURCE	PAGE
Table 21	Host Regions of U.S. Study Abroad Students, 1993/94 – 2003/04	58
Table 22	Host Regions and Destinations of U.S. Study Abroad Students, 2002/03 & 2003/04	58
Table 23	Fields of Study of U.S. Study Abroad Students, 1993/94 – 2003/04	61
Table 24	Duration of U.S. Study Abroad, 1993/94 – 2003/04	61
Table 25	Profile of U.S. Study Abroad Students, 1993/94 – 2003/04	62
Table 26	Home Institutional Type and For-Credit Internships or Work Abroad, 2000/01 – 2003/04; Program Sponsorship, 1994/95 – 2003/04; Financial Support for U.S. Study Abroad Students, 2003/04	63
Table 27A	Institutions by Undergraduate Participation in Study Abroad: Top 20 Doctoral/Research Institutions, 2003/04	64
Table 27B	Institutions by Total Number of Study Abroad Students: Top 20 Doctoral/Research Institutions, 2003/04	64
Table 28A	Institutions by Undergraduate Participation in Study Abroad: Top 20 Master's Institutions, 2003/04	65
Table 28B	Institutions by Total Number of Study Abroad Students: Top 20 Master's Institutions, 2003/04	66
Table 29A	Institutions by Undergraduate Participation in Study Abroad: Top 20 Baccalaureate Institutions, 2003/04	67
Table 29B	Institutions by Total Number of Study Abroad Students: Top 20 Baccalaureate Institutions, 2003/04	68

PERCENT OF U.S. STUDY ABROAD STUDENTS

Host Region	1993/94	1994/95	1995/96	1996/97	1997/98	1998/99	1999/00	2000/01	2001/02	2002/03	2003/04
Africa	1.9	2.2	2.3	2.6	2.7	2.8	2.8	2.9	2.9	2.8	3.0
Asia	6.5	6.4	6.4	6.1	6.0	6.0	6.2	6.0	6.8	5.6	6.9
Europe	67.4	65.5	64.8	64.5	63.7	62.7	62.4	63.1	62.6	62.9	60.9
Latin America	13.4	13.7	15.4	15.3	15.6	15.0	14.0	14.5	14.5	15.3	15.2
Middle East	2.8	3.3	2.1	1.9	2.0	2.8	2.9	1.1	0.8	0.4	0.5
North America *	0.7	0.7	0.7	0.7	0.9	0.7	0.9	0.7	0.8	0.7	0.6
Oceania	3.4	4.3	4.4	4.4	4.4	4.9	5.0	6.0	6.8	7.3	7.4
Multiple Regions	3.8	3.8	4.0	4.6	4.8	5.2	5.8	5.6	4.9	5.1	5.5
Total	**76,302**	**84,403**	**89,242**	**99,448**	**113,959**	**129,770**	**143,590**	**154,168**	**160,920**	**174,629**	**191,321**

* Includes Antarctica after 2001/02

21   HOST REGIONS OF STUDY ABROAD STUDENTS, 1993/94 – 2003/04

Destination	2002/03	2003/04	% Change	Destination	2002/03	2003/04	% Change
AFRICA	**4,827**	**5,699**	**18.1**	Gabon	3	1	-66.7
Africa, Unspecified	1	0	-100.0				
				North Africa	**495**	**882**	**78.2**
East Africa	**1,209**	**1,120**	**-7.4**	Egypt	303	573	89.1
Angola	0	1	-	Morocco	191	298	56.0
Eritrea	12	1	-91.7	Western Sahara	0	0	-
Ethiopia	26	26	0.0	Tunisia	0	11	-
Kenya	625	387	-38.1	North Africa, Unspecified	1	0	-100.0
Madagascar	15	62	313.3				
Malawi	9	12	33.3	**Southern Africa**	**1,811**	**2,219**	**22.5**
Mauritius	1	2	100.0	Botswana	42	80	90.5
Mozambique	29	42	44.8	Lesotho	34	28	-17.6
Reunion	0	3	-	Namibia	120	97	-19.2
Rwanda	6	10	66.7	South Africa	1,594	2,009	26.0
Somalia	-	1	-	Swaziland	21	5	-76.2
Tanzania	347	373	7.5	Southern Africa, Unspec.	0	0	-
Uganda	85	141	65.9				
Zambia	24	50	108.3	**West Africa**	**1,234**	**1,400**	**13.5**
Zimbabwe	29	9	-69.0	Benin	14	15	7.1
East Africa, Unspecified	1	0	-100.0	Burkina Faso	7	28	300.0
				Côte d'Ivoire	0	2	-
Central Africa	**77**	**78**	**1.3**	Gambia	22	34	54.5
Cameroon	66	74	12.1	Ghana	805	909	12.9
Central African Republic	0	0	-	Guinea	0	2	-
Chad	0	0	-	Liberia	1	2	100.0
Congo	1	0	-100.0	Mali	31	66	112.9
Congo (Former Zaire)	0	1	-	Mauritania	4	3	-25.0
Equatorial Guinea	7	2	-71.4	Niger	23	14	-39.1

22   HOST REGIONS AND DESTINATIONS OF U.S. STUDY ABROAD STUDENTS, 2002/03 & 2003/04

Destination	2002/03	2003/04	% Change
Nigeria	24	29	20.8
Senegal	286	280	-2.1
Sierra Leone	7	0	-100.0
Togo	7	16	128.6
West Africa, Unspecified	3	0	-100.0
ASIA	**9,751**	**13,213**	**35.5**
Asia, Unspecified	0	0	
East Asia	**7,322**	**10,075**	**37.6**
China	2,493	4,737	90.0
Hong Kong	458	487	6.3
Japan	3,457	3,707	7.2
Korea, Dem. People's Rep.	0	0	-
Korea, Republic of	739	881	19.2
Macau	0	0	-
Mongolia	27	68	151.9
Taiwan	148	195	31.8
South & Central Asia	**987**	**1,373**	**39.1**
Afghanistan	2	0	-100.0
Bangladesh	21	24	14.3
Bhutan	1	11	1,000.0
India	703	1,157	64.6
Indonesia	26	24	-7.7
Kazakhstan	2	10	400.0
Kyrgyzstan	2	0	-100.0
Nepal	142	98	-31.0
Pakistan	9	5	-44.4
Sri Lanka	72	32	-55.6
Tajikistan	1	1	0.0
Uzbekistan	6	11	83.3
Southeast Asia	**1,442**	**1,765**	**22.4**
Cambodia	12	43	258.3
East Timor	0	17	-
Laos	2	1	-50.0
Malaysia	47	43	-8.5
Myanmar	1	2	100.0
Philippines	124	165	33.1
Singapore	176	263	49.4
Thailand	794	948	19.4
Vietnam	286	283	-1.0
EUROPE	**109,907**	**116,446**	**5.9**
Europe, Unspecified	0	0	-
Eastern Europe	**5,017**	**5,498**	**9.6**
Albania	6	3	-50.0

Destination	2002/03	2003/04	% Change
Armenia	3	5	66.7
Azerbaijan	1	0	-100.0
Belarus	12	11	-8.3
Bosnia & Herzegovina	15	20	33.3
Bulgaria	36	28	-22.2
Croatia	41	68	65.9
Czech Republic	1,997	2,089	4.6
Estonia	15	33	120.0
Georgia	4	33	725.0
Hungary	562	654	16.4
Latvia	4	3	-25.0
Lithuania	16	27	68.8
Macedonia	15	1	-93.3
Moldova	4	0	-100.0
Poland	426	418	-1.9
Romania	97	136	40.2
Russia	1,521	1,797	18.1
Serbia & Montenegro/Kosovo	-	14	-
Slovakia	29	2	-93.1
Slovenia	26	18	-30.8
Ukraine	123	135	9.8
U.S.S.R., Former	-	1	-
Yugoslavia, Former	64	2	-96.9
E. Europe, Unspecified	0	0	-
Western Europe	**104,890**	**110,948**	**5.8**
Austria	2,798	2,444	-12.7
Belgium	890	901	1.2
Denmark	1,127	1,434	27.2
Finland	272	136	-50.0
France	13,080	13,718	4.9
Germany	5,587	5,985	7.1
Gibraltar	0	6	-
Greece	2,011	2,099	4.4
Iceland	134	117	-12.7
Ireland	4,892	5,198	6.3
Italy	18,936	21,922	15.8
Liechtenstein	1	0	-100.0
Luxembourg	343	420	22.4
Malta	67	86	28.4
Monaco	10	29	190.0
Netherlands	1,792	1,686	-5.9
Norway	270	243	-10.0
Portugal	143	80	-44.1
Spain	18,865	20,080	6.4
Sweden	818	830	1.5
Switzerland	1,148	1,280	11.5
United Kingdom	31,706	32,237	1.7
Vatican City	0	17	-

22 (cont'd) HOST REGIONS AND DESTINATIONS OF U.S. STUDY ABROAD STUDENTS, 2002/03 & 2003/04

Destination	2002/03	2003/04	% Change	Destination	2002/03	2003/04	% Change
W. Europe, Unspecified	0	0	-	Paraguay	59	75	27.1
				Peru	599	624	4.2
LATIN AMERICA	**26,643**	**29,053**	**9.0**	Suriname	0	14	-
Latin America, Unspec.	0	0	-	Uruguay	59	108	83.1
				Venezuela	57	81	42.1
Caribbean	**4,075**	**4,696**	**15.2**	S. America, Unspecified	0	0	-
Anguilla	13	1	-92.3				
Aruba	11	0	-100.0	**MIDDLE EAST**	**648**	**1,050**	**62.0**
Antigua	0	11	-	Bahrain	0	3	-
Bahamas	535	508	-5.0	Cyprus	10	38	280.0
Barbados	162	183	13.0	Iran	1	1	0.0
British Virgin Islands	119	140	17.6	Israel	340	665	95.6
Cayman Islands	43	15	-65.1	Jordan	29	65	124.1
Cuba	1,474	2,148	45.7	Kuwait	6	3	-50.0
Dominica	0	60	-	Lebanon	14	23	64.3
Dominican Republic	651	705	8.3	Oman	0	1	-
Grenada	0	26	-	Palestinian Authority	0	1	-
Guadeloupe	22	41	86.4	Qatar	0	2	-
Haiti	92	48	-47.8	Saudi Arabia	2	2	0.0
Jamaica	539	435	-19.3	Syria	4	19	375.0
Martinique	73	89	21.9	Turkey	228	200	-12.3
Montserrat	0	0	-	United Arab Emirates	12	20	66.7
Netherlands Antilles	13	34	161.5	Yemen	1	7	600.0
St. Kitts-Nevis	12	14	16.7	Middle East, Unspecified	1	0	-100.0
St. Lucia	0	1	-				
St. Vincent	6	16	166.7	**NORTH AMERICA**	**1,251**	**1,112**	**-11.1**
Trinidad & Tobago	107	161	50.5	Bermuda	57	58	1.8
Turks & Caicos Islands	19	40	110.5	Canada	1,194	1,054	-11.7
Windward Islands	0	0	-				
Caribbean, Unspecified	184	20	-89.1	**ANTARCTICA**	**18**	**24**	**33.3**
Central America & Mexico	**15,859**	**16,472**	**3.9**	**OCEANIA**	**12,749**	**14,113**	**10.7**
Belize	1,363	823	-39.6	Australia	10,691	11,418	6.8
Costa Rica	4,296	4,510	5.0	Cook Islands	1	2	100.0
El Salvador	117	232	98.3	Fed. States of Micronesia	16	15	-6.3
Guatemala	446	646	44.8	Fiji	66	132	100.0
Honduras	462	430	-6.9	French Polynesia	7	100	1,328.6
Mexico	8,775	9,293	5.9	Marshall Islands	8	6	-25.0
Nicaragua	290	343	18.3	New Zealand	1,917	2,369	23.6
Panama	109	195	78.9	Palau	0	0	-
C. America & Mexico, Unspec.	1	0	-100.0	Papua New Guinea	0	6	-
				Solomon Islands	-	1	-
South America	**6,709**	**7,885**	**17.5**	Tonga	0	26	-
Argentina	868	1,315	51.5	Vanuatu	4	2	-50.0
Bolivia	159	234	47.2	Western Samoa	25	36	44.0
Brazil	1,345	1,554	15.5	Pacific Islands, Unspec.	14	0	-100.0
Chile	1,944	2,135	9.8				
Colombia	15	20	33.3	**MULTI-DESTINATION**	**8,835**	**10,611**	**20.1**
Ecuador	1,567	1,678	7.1				
French Guiana	0	6	-	**TOTAL**	**174,629**	**191,321**	**9.6**
Guyana	37	41	10.8				

PERCENT OF U.S. STUDY ABROAD STUDENTS

Field of Study	1993/94	1994/95	1995/96	1996/97	1997/98*	1998/99	1999/00	2000/01	2001/02	2002/03	2003/04
Social Sciences	-	-	-	-	-	20.3	20.1	20.3	21.9	21.3	22.6
Business & Management	13.6	13.5	13.9	14.6	15.6	17.7	17.7	18.1	17.6	17.7	17.5
Humanities	-	-	-	-	-	14.6	14.5	14.5	13.8	13.3	13.3
Other	7.7	6.4	7.5	7.8	4.8	5.6	5.1	4.9	5.2	6.4	7.8
Fine or Applied Arts	7.7	9.0	6.8	7.1	7.7	8.0	8.6	8.5	8.5	9.0	7.6
Foreign Languages	11.3	10.3	10.7	9.3	8.0	8.1	8.2	8.2	8.5	7.9	7.5
Physical Sciences	5.3	6.8	6.8	6.8	7.0	7.4	7.4	7.1	7.6	7.1	7.1
Education	4.0	3.8	3.7	4.3	4.5	4.2	4.2	4.4	3.9	4.1	4.1
Health Sciences	1.7	2.1	2.3	2.7	3.2	3.8	2.8	3.2	3.0	3.1	3.4
Undeclared	3.6	3.3	3.9	3.9	4.2	4.3	5.1	4.5	3.8	3.5	3.4
Engineering	2.3	2.2	2.1	1.9	2.7	2.8	2.9	2.7	2.9	2.9	2.9
Math or Computer Sciences	1.1	1.2	1.3	1.6	1.6	1.8	2.0	2.0	2.2	2.4	1.7
Agriculture	0.9	0.7	1.0	1.2	1.5	1.4	1.4	1.6	1.1	1.5	1.2
Social Sciences & Humanities	37.1	36.6	35.2	34.0	34.8	-	-	-	-	-	-
Dual Major	3.6	4.1	4.7	4.9	4.3	-	-	-	-	-	-
Total	**76,302**	**84,403**	**89,242**	**99,448**	**113,959**	**129,770**	**143,590**	**154,168**	**160,920**	**174,629**	**191,321**

*Social Sciences & Humanities were combined until 1998/99.

23   FIELDS OF STUDY OF U.S. STUDY ABROAD STUDENTS, 1993/94 – 2003/04

PERCENT OF U.S. STUDY ABROAD STUDENTS

Duration of Study	1993/94	1994/95	1995/96	1996/97	1997/98	1998/99	1999/00	2000/01	2001/02	2002/03	2003/04
One Semester	37.2	39.4	39.4	40.2	38.4	39.8	38.1	38.5	39.0	40.3	38.1
Summer Term	30.9	30.0	31.4	32.8	33.8	34.6	34.2	33.7	34.4	32.7	37.0
Fewer Than 8 Weeks	1.7	2.5	3.5	3.3	4.2	4.8	7.3	7.4	7.3	9.4	8.9
Academic Year	14.3	14.0	12.1	10.7	9.5	8.6	8.2	7.3	7.8	6.7	6.0
January Term	5.6	6.9	5.6	6.8	6.6	6.5	6.0	7.0	6.0	5.6	5.7
One Quarter	6.3	4.8	5.1	4.0	4.8	4.0	4.7	4.1	3.9	3.8	3.3
Two Quarters	2.0	1.1	0.9	0.9	1.1	0.6	0.7	0.6	0.5	0.4	0.5
Other	1.4	0.9	1.3	1.2	1.0	0.8	0.4	0.9	0.6	0.6	0.3
Calendar Year	0.5	0.5	0.7	0.2	0.5	0.2	0.4	0.6	0.5	0.5	0.2
Total	**76,302**	**84,403**	**89,242**	**99,448**	**113,959**	**129,770**	**143,590**	**154,168**	**160,920**	**174,629**	**191,321**

24   DURATION OF U.S. STUDY ABROAD, 1993/94 – 2003/04

PERCENT OF U.S. STUDY ABROAD STUDENTS

	1993/94	1994/95	1995/96	1996/97	1997/98	1998/99	1999/00	2000/01	2001/02	2002/03	2003/04
Academic level											
Junior	40.6	43.0	41.6	41.3	42.2	40.3	39.8	38.9	40.7	38.0	34.7
Senior	15.6	16.3	16.2	18.3	17.7	19.0	17.7	20.0	20.4	20.2	19.3
Bachelor's, Unspecified	19.1	17.5	18.1	14.7	13.2	13.3	15.6	13.5	11.0	15.3	16.3
Sophomore	11.8	10.8	12.1	12.8	13.4	13.2	13.6	14.0	13.6	11.8	12.0
Other	0.8	1.5	0.7	0.8	0.5	1.1	1.0	1.1	0.8	0.7	4.2
Master's	4.0	4.1	3.7	4.2	5.1	4.5	5.0	4.5	4.7	4.8	4.1
Freshman	3.5	2.5	2.0	2.4	2.7	2.5	3.2	3.1	3.2	2.9	3.0
Graduate, Unspecified	2.3	2.6	3.2	3.3	2.6	3.2	2.7	3.1	3.3	3.4	2.4
Associate's	1.6	1.3	2.0	1.9	2.3	2.5	0.9	0.9	1.5	2.1	1.6
Graduate, Professional*	-	-	-	-	-	-	-	-	-	-	1.6
Doctoral	0.7	0.5	0.4	0.3	0.4	0.5	0.6	0.7	0.7	0.9	0.5
Sex											
Female	62.9	62.2	65.3	64.9	64.8	65.2	64.6	65.0	64.9	64.7	65.6
Male	37.1	37.8	34.7	35.1	35.2	34.8	35.4	35.0	35.1	35.3	34.4
Race/Ethnicity											
Caucasian	83.8	86.4	84.4	83.9	84.5	85.0	83.7	84.3	82.9	83.2	83.7
Asian-American	5.0	4.9	5.1	5.0	4.8	4.4	4.8	5.4	5.8	6.0	6.1
Hispanic-American	5.0	4.5	5.0	5.1	5.5	5.2	5.0	5.4	5.4	5.1	5.0
African-American	2.8	2.8	2.9	3.5	3.8	3.3	3.5	3.5	3.5	3.4	3.4
Multiracial	3.1	1.1	2.3	2.1	0.8	1.2	0.9	0.9	2	1.8	1.3
Native American	0.3	0.3	0.3	0.3	0.6	0.9	0.5	0.5	0.4	0.5	0.5
Visa Students*	-	-	-	-	-	-	1.6	-	-	-	-
TOTAL	**76,302**	**84,403**	**89,242**	**99,448**	**113,959**	**129,770**	**143,590**	**154,168**	**160,920**	**174,629**	**191,231**

* Captured for the first time in 2003/04

** Separate data on visa students collected in 1999/00

25   PROFILE OF U.S. STUDY ABROAD STUDENTS, 1993/94 – 2003/04

Carnegie Category	2000/01 %	2001/02 %	2002/03 %	2003/04 %	2003/04 Avg. # of Institutions
Doctoral/Research Extensive & Intensive	57.9	58.6	60.1	59.7	198
Master's I & II	20.5	20.5	20.5	20.4	280
Baccalaureate	18.0	17.6	16.6	16.0	240
Associate's	2.4	2.2	2.1	3.0	123
Specialized	1.2	1.0	0.8	0.8	46
Total Students	**154,168**	**160,920**	**174,629**	**191,321**	

For-Credit Internships or Work Abroad by Carnegie Type	2000/01 %	2000/01 # of Institutions	2001/02 %	2001/02 # of Institutions	2002/03 %	2002/03 # of Institutions	2003/04 %	2003/04 # of Institutions
Doctoral/Research Extensive & Intensive	51.1	85	56.7	107	52.1	100	62.9	99
Master's I & II	21.8	110	17.0	112	24.1	103	16.5	93
Baccalaureate	24.4	86	19.1	86	19.3	98	17.3	93
Associate's	0.5	5	1.9	7	2.3	11	1.4	9
Specialized	2.3	10	5.3	8	2.1	9	1.8	6
Total Students/Institutions	**6,950**	**296**	**7,331**	**320**	**8,477**	**321**	**8,021**	**300**

Program Sponsorship	1994/95 %	1995/96 %	1996/97 %	1997/98 %	1998/99 %	1999/00 %	2000/01 %	2001/02 %	2002/03 %	2003/04 %
Solely Own Institution	71.2	71.9	72.9	74.1	73.9	73.9	72.3	73.1	71.6	72.6
Other Institutions/Organizations	28.8	28.1	27.1	25.9	26.1	26.1	27.7	26.9	28.3	27.4
Total Students	**84,403**	**89,242**	**99,448**	**113,959**	**129,770**	**143,590**	**154,168**	**160,920**	**174,629**	**191,321**

Financial Support	2003/04 (%) Institution's Own Programs	2003/04 (%) Institution-Sponsored Programs	2003/04 (%) Other Programs
Federal Aid	92.6	86.2	44.2
State Aid	88.8	78.9	35.1
Need-Based Institutional Aid	87.3	70.7	17.0
Merit-Based Institutional Aid	86.8	68.4	18.1
Other Aid	84.9	66.1	27.7
Number of Responding Institutions	**583**	**549**	**412**

26 HOME INSTITUTIONAL TYPE AND FOR-CREDIT INTERNSHIPS OR WORK ABROAD, 2000/01 – 2003/04; PROGRAM SPONSORSHIP, 1994/95 – 2003/04; FINANCIAL SUPPORT FOR U.S. STUDY ABROAD STUDENTS, 2003/04

Rank	Institution	City	State	Study Abroad Students	Undergraduate Study Abroad Students	Total UG Degrees Conferred IPEDS 2003	Estimated % UG Participation In Study Abroad
1	University of St. Thomas	St. Paul	MN	753	662	1,075	61.6
2	Pepperdine University	Malibu	CA	694	492	800	61.5
3	Georgetown University	Washington	DC	1,323	984	1,670	58.9
4	Wake Forest University	Winston-Salem	NC	599	588	1,000	58.8
5	Dartmouth College	Hanover	NH	618	618	1,064	58.1
6	University of Notre Dame	Notre Dame	IN	1,284	1,099	2,052	53.6
7	Duke University	Durham	NC	902	761	1,539	49.4
8	American University	Washington	DC	751	613	1,291	47.5
9	University of Denver	Denver	CO	633	437	931	46.9
10	Worcester Polytechnic Institute	Worcester	MA	269	269	605	44.5
11	George Washington University	Washington	DC	919	892	2,128	41.9
12	Emory University	Atlanta	GA	800	687	1,720	39.9
13	Tufts University	Medford	MA	565	529	1,336	39.6
14	Boston College	Chestnut Hill	MA	993	874	2,223	39.3
15	Stanford University	Stanford	CA	665	665	1,713	38.8
16	University of Delaware	Newark	DE	1,303	1,277	3,402	37.5
17	U. of North Carolina at Chapel Hill	Chapel Hill	NC	1,660	1,362	3,715	36.7
18	U. of Virginia, Main Campus	Charlottesville	VA	1,427	1,153	3,207	36.0
19	Syracuse University	Syracuse	NY	1,133	1,005	2,804	35.8
20	Boston University	Boston	MA	1,482	1,391	3,992	34.8

Note: Study abroad participation rates were calculated only for institutions that provided academic level data.

27A   INSTITUTIONS BY UNDERGRADUATE PARTICIPATION IN STUDY ABROAD:
TOP 20 DOCTORAL/RESEARCH INSTITUTIONS, 2003/04

Rank	Institution	City	State	Study Abroad Students
1	New York University	New York	NY	2,475
2	Michigan State University	East Lansing	MI	2,269
3	University of California – Los Angeles	Los Angeles	CA	2,034
4	University of Texas at Austin	Austin	TX	2,011
5	Penn State University – University Park	University Park	PA	1,874
6	University of North Carolina at Chapel Hill	Chapel Hill	NC	1,657
7	University of Minnesota – Twin Cities	Minneapolis	MN	1,644
8	University of Wisconsin – Madison	Madison	WI	1,609
9	University of Georgia	Athens	GA	1,595
10	University of Arizona	Tucson	AZ	1,591
11	University of Florida	Gainesville	FL	1,537
12	University of Pennsylvania	Philadelphia	PA	1,510
13	Boston University	Boston	MA	1,482
14	University of Illinois at Urbana-Champaign	Champaign	IL	1,456
15	University of Washington	Seattle	WA	1,454

27B   INSTITUTIONS BY TOTAL NUMBER OF STUDY ABROAD STUDENTS:
TOP 20 DOCTORAL/RESEARCH INSTITUTIONS, 2003/04

ank	Institution	City	State	Study Abroad Students
6	Indiana University at Bloomington	Bloomington	IN	1,443
7	University of Virginia, Main Campus	Charlottesville	VA	1,427
8	Arizona State University	Tempe	AZ	1,409
9	The Ohio State University, Main Campus	Columbus	OH	1,399
0	Brigham Young University	Provo	UT	1,335

7B   (cont'd) INSTITUTIONS BY TOTAL NUMBER OF STUDY ABROAD STUDENTS: TOP 20 DOCTORAL/RESEARCH INSTITUTIONS, 2003/04

Rank	Institution	City	State	Study Abroad Students	Undergraduate Study Abroad Students	Total UG Degrees Conferred IPEDS 2003	Estimated % UG Participation In Study Abroad
1	Lynn University	Boca Raton	FL	560	551	356	154.8
2	Elon University	Elon College	NC	836	827	889	93.0
3	Queens University of Charlotte	Charlotte	NC	161	161	219	73.5
4	Arcadia University	Glenside	PA	229	217	304	71.4
5	University of Dubuque	Dubuque	IA	95	95	137	69.3
6	Warren Wilson College	Ashville	NC	103	103	154	66.9
7	University of Evansville	Evansville	IN	266	262	452	58.0
8	University of Richmond	Richmond	VA	525	445	770	57.8
9	Loyola College in Maryland	Baltimore	MD	409	409	802	51.0
10	Truman State University	Kirksville	MO	544	544	1,114	48.8
11	Pacific Lutheran University	Tacoma	WA	348	348	723	48.1
12	University of Redlands	Redlands	CA	356	356	754	47.2
13	Gonzaga University	Spokane	WA	341	341	766	44.5
14	Whitworth College	Spokane	WA	218	210	473	44.4
15	Bethel University	St. Paul	MN	302	302	695	43.5
16	Baker University	Baldwin City	KS	69	69	165	41.8
17	Samford University	Birmingham	AL	284	250	642	38.9
18	Saint Michael's College	Colchester	VT	173	173	455	38.0
19	Saint Mary's College of California	Moraga	CA	278	278	804	34.6
20	Rollins College	Winter Park	FL	254	250	743	33.6

Note: Study abroad participation rates were calculated only for institutions that provided academic level data.

28A   INSTITUTIONS BY UNDERGRADUATE PARTICIPATION IN STUDY ABROAD: TOP 20 MASTER'S INSTITUTIONS, 2003/04

Rank	Institution	City	State	Study Abroad Students
1	Elon University	Elon	NC	836
2	James Madison University	Harrisonburg	VA	709
3	Villanova University	Villanova	PA	592
4	California Polytechnic State U. – San Luis Obispo	San Luis Obispo	CA	563
5	Lynn University	Boca Raton	FL	560
6	Truman State University	Kirksville	MO	544
7	University of Richmond	Richmond	VA	525
8	Appalachian State University	Boone	NC	480
9	St. Cloud State University	St. Cloud	MN	468
10	University of Wisconsin – Eau Claire	Eau Claire	WI	452
11	University of Northern Iowa	Cedar Falls	IA	449
12	Ithaca College	Ithaca	NY	430
13	College of Charleston	Charleston	SC	412
14	Loyola College in Maryland	Baltimore	MD	409
15	University of Minnesota – Duluth	Duluth	MN	392
16	Grand Valley State University	Allendale	MI	360
17	University of North Florida	Jacksonville	FL	358
18	University of Wisconsin – Stevens Point	Stevens Point	WI	357
19	University of Redlands	Redlands	CA	356
20	Texas State University – San Marcos	San Marcos	TX	349

28B   INSTITUTIONS BY TOTAL NUMBER OF STUDY ABROAD STUDENTS: TOP 20 MASTER'S INSTITUTIONS, 2003/04

Rank	Institution	City	State	Study Abroad Students	Undergraduate Study Abroad Students	Total UG Degrees Conferred IPEDS 2003	Estimated % UG Participation In Study Abroad
1	Lee University	Cleveland	TN	725	725	642	112.9
2	Wofford College	Spartanburg	SC	277	277	247	112.1
3	St. Olaf College	Northfield	MN	771	771	708	108.9
4	Eckerd College	St. Petersburg	FL	310	310	329	94.2
5	Illinois Wesleyan University	Bloomington	IL	433	433	462	93.7
6	Earlham College	Richmond	IN	226	226	249	90.8
7	Centre College	Danville	KY	227	227	258	88.0
8	Lewis & Clark College	Portland	OR	323	323	371	87.1
9	DePauw University	Greencastle	IN	446	446	522	85.4
10	Kalamazoo College	Kalamazoo	MI	238	238	285	83.5
11	Dickinson College	Carlisle	PA	419	419	512	81.8
12	Colgate University	Hamilton	NY	524	524	646	81.1
13	Colby College	Waterville	ME	392	392	486	80.7
14	Carleton College	Northfield	MN	359	359	455	78.9
15	Austin College	Sherman	TX	237	236	310	76.1
16	University of Dallas	Irving	TX	184	184	248	74.2
17	Goucher College	Baltimore	MD	200	200	272	73.5
18	Colorado College	Colorado Springs	CO	384	384	523	73.4
19	Concordia College – Moorhead	Moorhead	MN	411	411	583	70.5
20	Davidson College	Davidson	NC	290	290	426	68.1

Note: Study abroad participation rates were calculated only for institutions that provided academic level data.

29A INSTITUTIONS BY UNDERGRADUATE PARTICIPATION IN STUDY ABROAD: TOP 20 BACCALAUREATE INSTITUTIONS, 2003/04

Rank	Institution	City	State	Study Abroad Students
1	St. Olaf College	Northfield	MN	771
2	Lee University	Cleveland	TN	725
3	College of St Benedict/St John's University	Collegeville	MN	565
4	Colgate University	Hamilton	NY	524
5	Calvin College	Grand Rapids	MI	489
6	DePauw University	Greencastle	IN	446
7	Illinois Wesleyan University	Bloomington	IL	433
8	Dickinson College	Carlisle	PA	419
8	Gustavus Adolphus College	St. Peter	MN	419
10	SUNY – Fashion Institute of Technology	New York	NY	414
11	Concordia College – Moorhead	Moorhead	MN	411
12	Colby College	Waterville	ME	392
13	Bucknell University	Lewisburg	PA	389
14	Colorado College	Colorado Springs	CO	384
14	Lafayette College	Easton	PA	384
16	Carleton College	Northfield	MN	359
17	Evergreen State College	Olympia	WA	356
18	Messiah College	Grantham	PA	354
19	Luther College	Decorah	IA	345
19	Smith College	Northampton	MA	345

**29B INSTITUTIONS BY TOTAL NUMBER OF STUDY ABROAD STUDENTS:
TOP 20 BACCALAUREATE INSTITUTIONS, 2003/04**

INTENSIVE ENGLISH

IN THIS SECTION

TABLE	SOURCE	PAGE
Table 30	IEP Students and Student-Weeks by the Percentage of Students Intending to Continue Further (Non-IEP) Study in the U.S., 2004	70
Table 31	Leading Places of Origin of IEP Students, 2002 – 2004	70
Table 32	Regions and Places of Origin of IEP Students, 2004	71
Table 33	IEP Students by State, 2004	74
Table 34	IEP Students and Student-Weeks by Enrollment Status in Selected Leading States, 2004	75
Table 35	Top 15 Places of Origin of IEP Students in Selected Leading Host States, 2004	76
Table 36	IEP Students and Student-Weeks by Program Type and Affiliation, 2004	77

% of Students Intending Further Study	# of Programs	Average # of Students Per Program	Total Students All Programs	Average # of Student-Weeks Per Program	Total Student-Weeks All Programs
30% and Less	39	360	14,042	3,423	133,496
31% to 60%	39	279	10,865	3,261	127,179
61% and Greater	65	161	10,468	2,143	139,311
All Reporting Programs*	143	247	35,375	2,797	399,986
All Programs	194		44,565		490,122

*51 programs did not provide further study data.

30 IEP STUDENTS AND STUDENT-WEEKS BY THE PERCENTAGE OF STUDENTS INTENDING TO CONTINUE FURTHER (NON-IEP) STUDY IN THE U.S., 2004

Rank	Place of Origin	2002 Total Students	2003 Total Students	2004 Total Students	% Change 2002-2004	2002 Student-Weeks	2003 Student-Weeks	2004 Student-Weeks	% Change 2002-2004
	WORLD TOTAL	51,179	43,003	44,565	-12.9	565,174	495,939	490,122	-13.3
1	Japan	13,047	10,519	10,804	-17.2	145,602	122,084	113,358	-22.1
2	Korea, Republic of	10,000	10,412	10,386	3.9	129,341	132,965	127,591	-1.4
3	Taiwan	5,919	4,235	5,126	-13.4	64,114	52,707	54,774	-14.6
4	Brazil	2,363	1,359	1,402	-40.7	18,121	11,782	11,169	-38.4
5	Turkey	1,102	1,034	1,133	2.8	11,224	12,408	11,776	4.9
6	France	1,231	1,156	1,093	-11.2	8,530	10,231	8,008	-6.1
7	Thailand	1,245	943	1,088	-12.6	15,630	12,899	11,998	-23.2
8	China	1,048	796	1,026	-2.1	13,517	9,276	11,891	-12.0
9	Germany	1,199	849	950	-20.8	8,885	7,266	7,622	-14.2
10	Mexico	1,171	1,408	949	-19.0	8,096	8,034	11,958	47.7
11	Italy	936	883	917	-2.0	10,998	8,942	4,917	-55.3
12	Switzerland	1,564	732	729	-53.4	12,380	6,577	6,458	-47.8
13	Spain	539	728	721	33.8	5,142	6,200	5,348	4.0
14	Colombia	1,089	858	700	-35.7	13,309	10,850	8,777	-34.0
15	Venezuela	1,216	742	648	-26.7	14,637	8,800	7,506	-48.7
16	Hong Kong	157	130	366	133.1	2,022	1,711	5,158	155.1
17	Peru	298	269	342	14.8	3,700	3,218	3,783	2.3
18	Saudi Arabia	756	348	334	-55.8	11,997	5,466	4,586	-61.8
19	Russia	292	273	296	1.4	3,103	2,894	2,785	-10.2
20	Vietnam	179	245	292	63.1	2,350	2,857	4,578	94.8

31 LEADING PLACES OF ORIGIN OF IEP STUDENTS, 2002 – 2004

Place of Origin	2004 Students	2004 Student-Weeks	Place of Origin	2004 Students	2004 Student-Weeks
AFRICA	**756**	**9,660**	**West Africa**	**340**	**4,478**
			Benin	15	215
East Africa	**61**	**1,303**	Burkina Faso	24	238
Burundi	1	6	Cape Verde	3	32
Comoros	0	0	Côte d'Ivoire	57	879
Eritrea	3	109	Gambia	4	72
Ethiopia	21	272	Ghana	12	160
Kenya	10	160	Guinea	19	221
Madagascar	1	15	Guinea-Bissau	3	16
Malawi	3	85	Liberia	8	153
Mauritius	2	45	Mali	51	571
Mozambique	2	0	Mauritania	22	280
Rwanda	2	26	Niger	40	620
Somalia	4	50	Nigeria	21	246
Tanzania	8	481	Senegal	40	466
Uganda	0	0	Sierra Leone	2	26
Zambia	4	54	Togo	19	283
Zimbabwe	0	0	**ASIA**	**30,050**	**344,536**
Central Africa	**166**	**2,286**			
Angola	37	712	**East Asia**	**27,916**	**318,417**
Cameroon	45	450	China	1,026	11,891
Central African Republic	2	25	Hong Kong	366	5,158
Chad	12	155	Japan	10,804	113,358
Congo	19	241	Korea, Dem. People's Rep.	25	1,329
Congo (Former Zaire)	0	0	Korea, Republic of	10,386	127,591
Equatorial Guinea	21	382	Macau	48	1,366
Gabon	30	321	Mongolia	135	2,950
São Tomé & Príncipe	0	0	Taiwan	5,126	54,774
North Africa	**166**	**1,551**	**South & Central Asia**	**360**	**3,922**
Algeria	23	114	Afghanistan	73	353
Egypt	26	259	Bangladesh	13	197
Libya	6	42	Bhutan	3	49
Morocco	80	827	India	104	1,134
Sudan	13	162	Kazakhstan	43	495
Tunisia	18	147	Kyrgyzstan	7	147
			Nepal	21	447
Southern Africa	**23**	**42**	Pakistan	34	509
Botswana	19	14	Sri Lanka	7	88
Namibia	0	0	Tajikistan	25	148
South Africa	4	28	Turkmenistan	5	64
Swaziland	0	0	Uzbekistan	25	291

Place of Origin	2004 Students	2004 Student-Weeks	Place of Origin	2004 Students	2004 Student-Weeks
Southeast Asia	**1,774**	**22,197**	Lithuania	9	88
Brunei	0	0	Macedonia	4	18
Cambodia	39	656	Moldova	11	150
Indonesia	228	3,272	Poland	263	3,001
Laos	11	147	Romania	26	274
Malaysia	62	712	Russia	296	2,785
Myanmar	16	222	Slovakia	31	260
Philippines	29	395	Slovenia	11	71
Singapore	9	217	Ukraine	80	896
Thailand	1,088	11,998	Yugoslavia, Former	13	213
Vietnam	292	4,578			
			Western Europe	**4,926**	**38,380**
MIDDLE EAST	**2,105**	**24,254**	Andorra	1	4
Bahrain	6	91	Austria	101	672
Cyprus	10	290	Belgium	47	534
Iran	87	656	Denmark	34	345
Iraq	28	788	Finland	9	98
Israel	49	502	France	1,093	8,008
Jordan	62	666	Germany	950	7,622
Kuwait	131	1,745	Greece	17	144
Lebanon	16	180	Iceland	3	10
Oman	14	273	Ireland	2	36
Palestinian Authority	18	149	Italy	917	4,917
Qatar	14	218	Liechtenstein	4	26
Saudi Arabia	334	4,586	Luxembourg	1	8
Syria	31	344	Monaco	2	37
Turkey	1,133	11,776	Netherlands	35	431
United Arab Emirates	153	1,601	Norway	14	129
Yemen	19	389	Portugal	38	207
			San Marino	2	7
EUROPE	**6,002**	**49,668**	Spain	721	5,348
			Sweden	192	3,157
Eastern Europe	**1,076**	**11,288**	Switzerland	729	6,458
Albania	13	139	United Kingdom	13	182
Armenia	12	136	Vatican City	0	0
Azerbaijan	10	110	Malta	1	0
Belarus	12	176			
Bosnia & Herzegovina	9	112	**LATIN AMERICA**	**5,294**	**56,716**
Bulgaria	47	712			
Croatia	23	134	Caribbean	120	1,434
Czech Republic	78	708	Antigua	0	0
Estonia	9	96	Aruba	0	0
Georgia	31	274	Bahamas	0	0
Hungary	70	690	British Virgin Islands	1	23
Latvia	18	245	Cuba	11	120

32   (cont'd) REGIONS AND PLACES OF ORIGIN OF IEP STUDENTS, 2004

Place of Origin	2004 Students	2004 Student-Weeks	Place of Origin	2004 Students	2004 Student-Weeks
Dominican Republic	68	579	Ecuador	205	2,549
Grenada	1	18	Falkland Islands	0	0
Guadeloupe	1	0	Paraguay	50	446
Haiti	32	633	Peru	342	3,783
Jamaica	1	12	Suriname	1	18
Martinique	3	12	Uruguay	24	216
Montserrat	0	0	Venezuela	648	7,506
Netherlands Antilles	1	0			
St. Lucia	0	0	**NORTH AMERICA**	**50**	**708**
Trinidad & Tobago	1	37	Canada	50	708
Central America & Mexico	**1,276**	**15,852**	**OCEANIA**	**127**	**2,905**
Belize	1	36	Australia	7	65
Costa Rica	56	431	Fiji	24	502
El Salvador	43	563	French Polynesia	26	585
Guatemala	57	791	Kiribati	9	213
Honduras	31	391	New Caledonia	0	0
Mexico	949	11,958	New Zealand	5	98
Nicaragua	39	472	Papua New Guinea	3	88
Panama	100	1,210	Tonga	36	995
			Western Samoa	17	359
South America	**3,898**	**39,430**			
Argentina	210	1,879	**UNKNOWN**	**181**	**1,675**
Bolivia	90	992			
Brazil	1,402	11,169	**WORLD TOTAL**	**44,565**	**490,122**
Chile	226	2,095			
Colombia	700	8,777			

32 (cont'd) REGIONS AND PLACES OF ORIGIN OF IEP STUDENTS, 2004

State	Reporting Programs	Total Students	Total Student-Weeks
Alabama	1	272	3,908
Arkansas	2	147	2,353
Arizona	1	515	4,120
California	29	10,045	98,691
Colorado	7	741	9,786
Connecticut	4	180	2,492
District of Columbia	3	559	1,717
Delaware	1	731	9,696
Florida	12	2,428	22,198
Georgia	3	398	4,904
Guam	0	0	0
Hawaii	5	2,068	15,685
Idaho	2	92	340
Iowa	1	0	0
Illinois	6	1,790	20,430
Indiana	3	961	11,347
Kansas	3	546	7,461
Kentucky	2	182	1,612
Louisiana	1	0	0
Massachussetts	5	2,107	20,300
Maryland	2	322	4,837
Maine	1	26	391
Michigan	3	245	3,691
Minnesota	2	295	3,529
Missouri	4	295	4,192
North Carolina	2	260	3,823
North Dakota	2	23	334
Nebraska	1	400	0
New Mexico	0	0	0
Nevada	1	200	3,074
New Jersey	3	1,110	9,300
New York	16	4,295	38,172
Ohio	7	782	8,113
Oklahoma	5	910	10,608
Oregon	7	706	10,229
Pennsylvania	6	1,700	18,241
South Carolina	1	134	1,913
Tennessee	4	325	4,272
Texas	10	2,213	33,764
Utah	2	726	16,784
Vermont	1	300	2,086
Virginia	3	593	5,355
Washington	12	4,250	65,266
Wisconsin	4	422	1,369
West Virginia	3	268	3,715
Wyoming	1	3	24
U.S. TOTAL	**194**	**44,565**	**490,122**

33 IEP STUDENTS BY STATE, 2004

CALIFORNIA		NEW YORK	
	% of Students		**% of Students**
Part-Time	42.1	Part-Time	10.8
Full-Time	57.9	Full-Time	89.2
State Total	**10,045**	**State Total**	**4,295**
	% Student-Weeks		**% Student-Weeks**
Part-Time	37.3	Part-Time	12.1
Full-Time	62.7	Full-Time	87.9
State Total	**98,691**	**State Total**	**38,172**

TEXAS		FLORIDA	
	% of Students		**% of Students**
Part-Time	8.7	Part-Time	6.6
Full-Time	91.3	Full-Time	93.4
State Total	**2,213**	**State Total**	**2,428**
	% Student-Weeks		**% Student-Weeks**
Part-Time	15.2	Part-Time	6.6
Full-Time	84.8	Full-Time	93.4
State Total	**33,764**	**State Total**	**22,198**

* Full-time enrollment is 18 class-hours per week or more; part-time is fewer than 18 class-hours per week.

**34 IEP STUDENTS AND STUDENT-WEEKS BY ENROLLMENT STATUS
IN SELECTED LEADING STATES, 2004**

CALIFORNIA

Rank	Place of Origin	Students	Student-Weeks	% of Students
1	Japan	3,041	24,212	30.3
2	Korea, Republic of	2,119	18,022	21.1
3	Taiwan	1,697	12,995	16.9
4	Italy	398	1,530	4.0
5	Brazil	395	2,583	3.9
6	France	387	2,396	3.9
7	China	320	2,864	3.2
8	Thailand	316	2,000	3.1
9	Germany	305	2,739	3.0
10	Turkey	285	1,865	2.8
11	Switzerland	269	2,377	2.7
12	Spain	212	1,176	2.1
13	Sweden	157	2,624	1.6
14	Mexico	121	1,340	1.2
15	Vietnam	75	997	0.7
	State Total	**10,045**	**98,691**	

NEW YORK

Rank	Place of Origin	Students	Student-Weeks	% of Students
1	Korea, Republic of	1,100	12,445	25.6
2	Japan	872	9,072	20.3
3	Taiwan	459	4,366	10.7
4	Germany	343	1,428	8.0
5	Turkey	184	1,790	4.3
6	Italy	176	857	4.1
7	France	171	955	4.0
8	Spain	150	746	3.5
9	Brazil	114	661	2.7
10	Switzerland	69	483	1.6
11	China	53	489	1.2
12	Colombia	50	502	1.2
13	Thailand	46	417	1.1
14	Poland	43	304	1.0
15	Mexico	35	286	0.8
	State Total	**4,295**	**38,172**	

TEXAS

Rank	Place of Origin	Students	Student-Weeks	% of Students
1	Korea, Republic of	588	7,975	26.6
2	Taiwan	295	3,978	13.3
3	Mexico	227	2,601	10.3
4	Japan	203	2,721	9.2
5	Turkey	83	998	3.8
6	Colombia	77	1,206	3.5
7	Venezuela	77	1,216	3.5
8	Brazil	72	736	3.3
9	Thailand	54	731	2.4
10	China	51	648	2.3
11	Peru	40	513	1.8
12	Saudi Arabia	25	178	1.1
13	Spain	22	224	1.0
14	France	21	213	0.9
15	Hong Kong	19	40	0.9
	State Total	**2,213**	**33,764**	

FLORIDA

Rank	Place of Origin	Students	Student-Weeks	% of Students
1	Korea, Republic of	339	4,991	14.0
2	Japan	276	3,163	11.4
3	Venezuela	204	1,891	8.4
4	Brazil	181	1,299	7.5
5	France	136	850	5.6
6	Taiwan	124	990	5.1
7	Turkey	117	744	4.8
8	Colombia	93	980	3.8
9	Peru	92	222	3.8
10	Italy	65	317	2.7
11	Spain	62	363	2.6
12	Switzerland	62	807	2.6
13	Argentina	44	300	1.8
14	Ecuador	42	528	1.7
15	Saudi Arabia	38	607	1.6
	State Total	**2,428**	**22,198**	

35 TOP 15 PLACES OF ORIGIN OF IEP STUDENTS IN SELECTED LEADING HOST STATES, 2004

	# of Programs	Total # of Students	Total Taking Less Than 18 Hours	Total Taking More Than 18 Hours	Total # of Student-Weeks	Student-Weeks Less Than 18 Hours	Student-Weeks More Than 18 Hours
Program Type/Membership							
Independent for-profit affiliated by contract with an institution of higher education	67	11,281	1,363	9,918	113,657	11,647	102,010
Independent for-profit not affiliated by contract with an institution of higher education	21	8,547	3,573	4,974	67,281	17,652	49,629
Independent not-for-profit affiliated by contract with an institution of higher education	10	1,874	283	1,591	30,988	4,203	26,785
Independent not-for-profit not affiliated by contract with an institution of higher education	3	528	206	322	10,945	6,580	4,365
Private college- or university-governed	28	4,608	1,381	3,227	42,692	8,375	34,317
Public college- or university-governed	65	17,727	3,556	14,171	224,559	49,357	175,202
Membership Affiliation							
AAIEP Only	113	27,492	7,490	20,002	267,301	56,366	210,935
UCIEP Only	9	3,060	828	2,232	30,542	9,621	20,921
Both AAIEP & UCIEP	28	6,809	1,118	5,691	89,383	20,552	68,831
Neither	44	7,204	2,409	4,795	102,896	30,588	72,308
ALL PROGRAMS	**194**	**44,565**	**11,845**	**32,720**	**490,122**	**117,127**	**372,995**

36   IEP STUDENTS AND STUDENT-WEEKS BY PROGRAM TYPE AND AFFILIATION, 2004

INTERNATIONAL SCHOLARS

IN THIS SECTION

TABLE	SOURCE	PAGE
Table 37	International Scholar Totals by Place of Origin, 2003/04 & 2004/05	80
Table 38	Leading Institutions Hosting International Scholars, 2003/04 & 2004/05	83
Table 39	International Scholars by State, 1994/95 − 2004/05	84
Table 40	Visa Status, Sex, and Primary Function of International Scholars, 1994/95 − 2004/05	85
Table 41	Major Field of Specialization of International Scholars 1994/95 − 2004/05	86

Place of Origin	2003/04	2004/05	% Change
AFRICA	**2,257**	**2,338**	**3.6**
East Africa	**544**	**573**	**5.3**
Burundi	1	2	100.0
Comoros	3	1	-66.7
Eritrea	8	5	-37.5
Ethiopia	63	70	11.1
Kenya	197	206	4.6
Madagascar	15	11	-26.7
Malawi	9	10	11.1
Mauritius	15	16	6.7
Mozambique	6	7	16.7
Rwanda	10	13	30.0
Somalia	4	4	0.0
Tanzania	56	66	17.9
Uganda	76	65	-14.5
Zambia	37	19	-48.6
Zimbabwe	44	78	77.3
Central Africa	**144**	**110**	**-23.6**
Angola	14	1	-92.9
Cameroon	62	79	27.4
Central African Republic	1	0	-100.0
Chad	32	2	-93.8
Congo	20	17	-15.0
Congo (Former Zaire)	5	4	-20.0
Equatorial Guinea	4	2	-50.0
Gabon	6	5	-16.7
São Tomé & Príncipe	0	0	-
North Africa	**648**	**744**	**14.8**
Algeria	63	75	19.0
Egypt	374	472	26.2
Libya	4	4	0.0
Morocco	106	106	0.0
Sudan	19	13	-31.6
Tunisia	82	74	-9.8
Southern Africa	**378**	**328**	**-13.2**
Botswana	15	11	-26.7
Lesotho	6	2	-66.7
Namibia	14	2	-85.7
South Africa	335	312	-6.9
Swaziland	8	1	-87.5

Place of Origin	2003/04	2004/05	% Change
West Africa	**543**	**583**	**7.4**
Benin	14	13	-7.1
Burkina Faso	14	12	-14.3
Côte d'Ivoire	19	16	-15.8
Gambia	10	17	70.0
Ghana	115	160	39.1
Guinea	3	2	-33.3
Liberia	6	12	100.0
Mali	20	23	15.0
Mauritania	4	4	0.0
Niger	14	5	-64.3
Nigeria	259	238	-8.1
Senegal	48	55	14.6
Sierra Leone	9	13	44.4
Togo	8	13	62.5
ASIA	**39,121**	**43,654**	**11.6**
East Asia	**29,382**	**32,874**	**11.9**
China	14,871	17,035	14.6
Hong Kong	182	304	67.0
Japan	5,627	5,623	-0.1
Korea, Dem. People's Rep.	25	14	-44.0
Korea, Republic of	7,290	8,301	13.9
Macau	3	6	100.0
Mongolia	37	48	29.7
Taiwan	1,347	1,543	14.6
South & Central Asia	**8,086**	**9,032**	**11.7**
Afghanistan	3	8	166.7
Bangladesh	240	253	5.4
Bhutan	4	6	50.0
India	6,809	7,755	13.9
Kazakhstan	61	62	1.6
Kyrgyzstan	49	33	-32.7
Maldives	1	0	-100.0
Nepal	105	118	12.4
Pakistan	551	494	-10.3
Sri Lanka	155	185	19.4
Tajikistan	20	16	-20.0
Turkmenistan	8	6	-25.0
Uzbekistan	80	96	20.0
Southeast Asia	**1,653**	**1,748**	**5.7**
Brunei	0	1	-
Cambodia	11	12	9.1

37 INTERNATIONAL SCHOLAR TOTALS BY PLACE OF ORIGIN, 2003/04 & 2004/05

Place of Origin	2003/04	2004/05	% Change
Indonesia	208	207	-0.5
Laos	3	5	66.7
Malaysia	176	166	-5.7
Myanmar	18	28	55.6
Philippines	318	372	17.0
Singapore	214	201	-6.1
Thailand	572	619	8.2
Vietnam	133	137	3.0
EUROPE	**26,728**	**27,975**	**4.7**
Eastern Europe	**6,603**	**6,849**	**3.7**
Albania	57	48	-15.8
Armenia	85	60	-29.4
Azerbaijan	44	37	-15.9
Belarus	81	103	27.2
Bosnia & Herzegovina	23	31	34.8
Bulgaria	308	318	3.2
Croatia	119	98	-17.6
Czech Republic	316	317	0.3
Estonia	38	43	13.2
Georgia	106	106	0.0
Hungary	399	417	4.5
Latvia	39	47	20.5
Lithuania	64	62	-3.1
Macedonia	38	39	2.6
Moldova	59	67	13.6
Poland	927	925	-0.2
Romania	575	674	17.2
Russia	2,403	2,420	0.7
Serbia & Montenegro/Kosovo	-	142	-
Slovakia	169	164	-3.0
Slovenia	40	65	62.5
Ukraine	531	549	3.4
Yugoslavia, Former	182	117	-35.7
Western Europe	**20,125**	**21,126**	**5.0**
Austria	347	375	8.1
Belgium	395	391	-1.0
Denmark	411	428	4.1
Finland	258	294	14.0
France	2,842	3,078	8.3
Germany	4,737	4,846	2.3
Gibraltar	0	1	-
Greece	537	544	1.3
Iceland	52	56	7.7

Place of Origin	2003/04	2004/05	% Change
Ireland	360	366	1.7
Italy	2,317	2,565	10.7
Liechtenstein	1	1	0.0
Luxembourg	15	16	6.7
Malta	9	12	33.3
Monaco	1	2	100.0
Netherlands	975	946	-3.0
Norway	307	316	2.9
Portugal	246	314	27.6
San Marino	1	0	-100.0
Spain	1,893	2,043	7.9
Sweden	642	686	6.9
Switzerland	662	661	-0.2
United Kingdom	3,117	3,185	2.2
LATIN AMERICA	**5,401**	**5,741**	**6.3**
Caribbean	**335**	**309**	**-7.8**
Antigua	4	10	150.0
Aruba	30	1	-96.7
Bahamas	34	31	-8.8
Barbados	24	19	-20.8
British Virgin Islands	3	1	-66.7
Cuba	16	30	87.5
Dominica	10	13	30.0
Dominican Republic	27	24	-11.1
Grenada	3	5	66.7
Guadeloupe	0	0	0.0
Haiti	19	19	0.0
Jamaica	69	78	13.0
Martinique	0	0	-
Montserrat	1	0	-100.0
Netherlands Antilles	27	4	-85.2
St. Kitts-Nevis	3	4	33.3
St. Lucia	3	2	-33.3
St. Vincent	3	2	-33.3
Trinidad & Tobago	59	66	11.9
Turks & Caicos Islands	0	0	-
Central America & Mexico	**1,288**	**1,426**	**10.7**
Belize	16	10	-37.5
Costa Rica	69	80	15.9
El Salvador	20	23	15.0
Guatemala	77	54	-29.9
Honduras	30	50	66.7
Mexico	1,032	1,158	12.2

37 (cont'd) INTERNATIONAL SCHOLAR TOTALS BY PLACE OF ORIGIN, 2003/04 & 2004/05

Place of Origin	2003/04	2004/05	% Change	Place of Origin	2003/04	2004/05	% Change
Nicaragua	9	14	55.6	Palestinian Authority	16	10	-37.5
Panama	35	37	5.7	Qatar	1	2	100.0
				Saudi Arabia	44	41	-6.8
South America	**3,778**	**4,006**	**6.0**	Syria	106	109	2.8
Argentina	820	825	0.6	Turkey	1,215	1,427	17.4
Bolivia	38	41	7.9	United Arab Emirates	21	7	-66.7
Brazil	1,341	1,499	11.8	Yemen	13	17	30.8
Chile	291	296	1.7				
Colombia	524	550	5.0	**NORTH AMERICA**	**4,128**	**4,267**	**3.4**
Ecuador	82	122	48.8	Bermuda	3	5	66.7
Guyana	16	14	-12.5	Canada	4,125	4,262	3.3
Paraguay	19	11	-42.1				
Peru	207	232	12.1	**OCEANIA**	**1,521**	**1,528**	**0.5**
Suriname	4	5	25.0	Australia	1,197	1,183	-1.2
Uruguay	101	117	15.8	Fiji	5	2	-60.0
Venezuela	335	294	-12.2	French Polynesia	1	2	100.0
				Kiribati	0	0	-
MIDDLE EAST	**3,692**	**4,127**	**11.8**	New Zealand	317	335	5.7
Bahrain	25	16	-36.0	Niue	0	0	-
Cyprus	63	63	0.0	Papua New Guinea	1	4	300.0
Iran	331	398	20.2	Tonga	0	0	-
Iraq	42	37	-11.9	Western Samoa	0	2	-
Israel	1,409	1,500	6.5				
Jordan	148	203	37.2	**STATELESS**	**57**	**4**	**-93.0**
Kuwait	30	25	-16.7				
Lebanon	222	262	18.0	**WORLD TOTAL**	**82,905**	**89,634**	**8.1**
Oman	6	10	66.7				

37 (cont'd) INTERNATIONAL SCHOLAR TOTALS BY PLACE OF ORIGIN, 2003/04 & 2004/05

Rank	Institution	City	State	2003/04	2004/05
1	Harvard University	Cambridge	MA	3,029	3,367
2	University of California – Los Angeles	Los Angeles	CA	2,130	2,159
3	University of California – Berkeley	Berkeley	CA	1,960	2,107
4	University of California – San Diego	La Jolla	CA	1,949	2,075
5	Columbia University	New York	NY	1,916	1,991
6	University of Pennsylvania	Philadelphia	PA	1,938	1,938 L
7	University of Florida	Gainesville	FL	1,704	1,886
8	Yale University	New Haven	CT	1,770	1,874
9	Massachusetts Institute of Technology	Cambridge	MA	1,567	1,687
10	University of Washington	Seattle	WA	1,557	1,625
11	University of California – Irvine	Irvine	CA	1,478	1,607
12	Stanford University	Stanford	CA	1,642	1,595
13	The Ohio State University, Main Campus	Columbus	OH	1,520	1,570
14	University of California – Davis	Davis	CA	1,356	1,516
15	University of Illinois at Urbana-Champaign	Champaign	IL	1,427	1,470
16	University of California – San Francisco	San Francisco	CA	1,600	1,394
17	Washington University in St. Louis	St. Louis	MO	1,195	1,336
18	Cornell University	Ithaca	NY	1,242	1,305
19	University of Southern California	Los Angeles	CA	1,280	1,303
20	Texas A&M University	College Station	TX	775	1,254
21	Michigan State University	East Lansing	MI	977	1,221
22	University of Minnesota – Twin Cities	Minneapolis	MN	1,241	1,196
23	University of Michigan	Ann Arbor	MI	1,291	1,188
24	Duke University & Medical Center	Durham	NC	1,120	1,187
25	Pennsylvania State University – University Park	University Park	PA	637	1,184
26	University of North Carolina at Chapel Hill	Chapel Hill	NC	1,047	1,183
27	University of Maryland College Park	College Park	MD	1,038	1,140
28	Boston University	Boston	MA	1,080	1,135
29	University of Texas at Austin	Austin	TX	946	1,022
30	University of Wisconsin – Madison	Madison	WI	1,177	1,011

L = estimated based on last year's total

38   LEADING INSTITUTIONS HOSTING INTERNATIONAL SCHOLARS, 2003/04 & 2004/05

State	1994/95 Total	1995/96 Total	1996/97 Total	1997/98 Total	1998/99 Total	1999/00 Total	2000/01 Total	2001/02 Total	2002/03 Total	2003/04 Total	2004/05 Total	% Change from 03/04
Alabama	652	591	659	765	507	763	898	893	979	960	895	-6.8
Alaska	50	24	31	31	0*	0*	0*	0*	0*	0*	0*	-
Arizona	515	835	887	889	1,095	1,199	1,191	1,168	1,308	1,121	1,111	-0.9
Arkansas	214	307	157	199	138	126	161	175	197	379	216	-43.0
California	10,314	11,723	10,485	11,530	13,311	13,641	13,365	16,236	14,097	15,313	16,101	5.1
Colorado	1,156	922	946	920	1,109	1,122	1,272	1,376	1,412	1,400	1,315	-6.1
Connecticut	33	985	1,040	1,100	1,060	1,321	1,360	1,834	1,637	1,770	1,874	5.9
Delaware	328	363	366	327	374	677	386	455	455	421	421	0.0
District of Columbia	731	779	742	544	741	776	648	610	511	525	545	3.8
Florida	1,820	1,661	1,822	1,858	1,770	2,114	2,436	2,552	2,427	2,987	3,409	14.1
Georgia	1,246	2,201	1,434	1,592	1,809	1,844	1,780	1,852	1,730	2,045	2,071	1.3
Hawaii	188	188	234	293	296	296	376	446	446	457	532	16.4
Idaho	46	321	272	76	64	103	113	136	167	141	31	-78.0
Illinois	2,374	1,741	2,847	2,892	3,379	3,545	4,048	4,392	4,144	2,849	3,599	26.3
Indiana	1,438	1,550	1,672	1,754	1,600	1,994	1,826	1,950	2,036	1,735	1,881	8.4
Iowa	774	922	1,139	941	1,260	1,276	1,500	1,441	1,511	1,105	1,885	70.6
Kansas	362	313	413	343	423	425	581	451	423	651	486	-25.3
Kentucky	368	445	482	517	580	412	600	635	387	580	637	9.8
Louisiana	539	505	486	591	567	851	626	713	743	746	596	-20.1
Maine	63	54	28	34	81	75	116	159	110	107	3	-97.2
Maryland	668	737	1,117	1,647	1,059	1,417	1,506	1,965	1,970	1,444	1,505	4.2
Massachusetts	5,185	5,274	5,044	5,219	5,184	5,181	6,180	6,340	5,858	6,798	7,164	5.4
Michigan	2,165	1,725	2,430	2,253	2,356	2,694	2,930	3,137	3,204	3,260	3,218	-1.3
Minnesota	1,227	1,231	1,197	1,255	1,281	1,260	1,271	1,475	1,348	1,312	1,196	-8.8
Mississippi	178	171	164	161	232	302	285	347	229	364	208	-42.9
Missouri	1,473	1,429	1,485	1,509	1,387	1,454	1,681	1,706	2,137	2,025	2,341	15.6
Montana	93	113	128	112	132	133	248	234	129	225	224	-0.4
Nebraska	300	244	357	207	538	312	537	599	594	655	687	4.9
Nevada	98	185	167	173	285	185	199	257	216	298	335	12.4
New Hampshire	195	240	234	324	355	443	468	437	440	494	536	8.5
New Jersey	919	520	472	558	630	564	1,209	1,195	1,223	1,516	1,366	-9.9
New Mexico	210	222	168	257	239	237	304	340	260	439	456	3.9
New York	4,599	4,067	4,311	4,468	5,262	5,309	5,728	5,847	6,246	6,009	6,450	7.3
North Carolina	1,424	1,463	1,414	1,776	1,684	1,968	2,145	2,581	2,929	2,944	3,164	7.5
North Dakota	53	57	98	87	85	91	139	129	230	256	182	-28.9
Ohio	1,862	1,920	2,103	2,525	2,500	2,646	2,559	2,330	2,311	2,187	3,370	54.1
Oklahoma	450	219	456	432	659	548	472	388	352	319	232	-27.3
Oregon	715	792	729	756	762	763	794	837	775	772	814	5.4

State	1994/95 Total	1995/96 Total	1996/97 Total	1997/98 Total	1998/99 Total	1999/00 Total	2000/01 Total	2001/02 Total	2002/03 Total	2003/04 Total	2004/05 Total	% Change from 03/04
Pennsylvania	3,681	3,277	4,012	3,858	4,357	4,557	4,655	5,463	5,517	5,020	5,741	14.4
Rhode Island	341	399	449	434	408	383	528	528	425	0*	0*	-
South Carolina	469	422	547	964	913	1,021	810	746	726	269	1,044	288.1
South Dakota	10	23	35	14	21	8	18	17	8	8	27	237.5
Tennessee	1,197	1,000	1,087	893	1,055	1,169	1,751	1,663	1,676	869	789	-9.2
Texas	3,574	3,243	3,616	3,636	4,288	4,686	4,349	4,885	5,502	4,956	5,824	17.5
Utah	448	383	505	511	558	567	669	492	393	389	749	92.5
Vermont	207	200	189	209	203	228	231	0*	0*	0*	0*	-
Virginia	1,015	1,017	1,042	1,191	1,427	1,423	1,553	1,438	1,227	1,128	879	-22.1
Washington	1,215	1,309	1,397	1,465	1,585	1,659	1,809	1,786	2,133	2,137	2,193	2.6
West Virginia	54	40	28	33	32	33	44	38	60	74	74	0.0
Wisconsin	750	888	1,077	1,243	730	652	1,191	1,247	1,281	1,261	1,179	-6.5
Wyoming	56	103	83	83	85	85	71	66	107	107	0*	-
Puerto Rico	32	60	71	45	45	33	34	28	55	78	79	1.3
U.S. TOTAL	58,074	59,403	62,354	65,494	70,501	74,571	79,651	86,015	84,281	82,905	89,634	8.1

*Data not provided

39 (cont'd) INTERNATIONAL SCHOLARS BY STATE, 1994/95 – 2004/05

Characteristic	PERCENT OF INTERNATIONAL SCHOLARS										
	1994/95	1995/96	1996/97	1997/98	1998/99	1999/00	2000/01	2001/02	2002/03	2003/04	2004/05
Visa Status											
J (All)	76.6	77.0	75.9	73.2	74.3	.	.	.	.	.	.
J-1	.	.	.	.	.	69.0	68.5	64.0	56.7	53.6	51.0
J-1 Other	..	.	.	.	.	2.6	2.3	2.7	3.7	2.5	3.0
H-1B	16.0	16.2	17.6	18.3	18.8	20.5	22.0	24.6	31.0	34.7	37.4
TN	..	.	.	.	.	1.5	1.6	1.6	1.3	2.3	1.4
O-1	..	.	.	.	.	0.8	1.1	1.2	1.1	0.9	0.8
Other	7.4	6.8	6.5	8.5	6.8	5.5	4.4	5.9	6.2	6.0	6.4
Sex											
Male	73.8	73.7	74.2	73.7	72.0	71.8	70.5	69.3	68.2	67.0	66.5
Female	26.2	26.3	25.8	26.3	28.0	28.2	29.5	30.7	31.8	33.0	33.5
Primary Function											
Research	80.7	82.6	81.9	83.1	81.0	76.5	79.2	77.2	74.2	75.8	73.2
Teaching	12.2	11.5	11.5	11.5	10.9	10.4	10.8	11.7	12.2	13.4	13.3
Both Research & Teaching	7.1	5.9	6.6	5.4	8.1	7.8	5.0	4.9	7.1	5.9	7.1
Other	.	.	.	.	.	5.3	5.0	6.2	6.5	5.0	6.4
TOTAL	58,074	59,403	62,354	65,494	70,501	74,571	79,651	86,015	84,281	82,905	89,634

40 VISA STATUS, SEX, AND PRIMARY FUNCTION OF INTERNATIONAL SCHOLARS, 1994/95 – 2004/05

Major Field of Specialization	PERCENT OF INTERNATIONAL SCHOLARS										
	1994/95	1995/96	1996/97	1997/98	1998/99	1999/00	2000/01	2001/02	2002/03	2003/04	2004/05
Health Sciences	28.6	27.6	27.1	26.9	26.2	23.8	26.9	27.4	25.0	20.8	21.9
Life & Biological Sciences	14.1	12.8	15.4	14.4	15.4	16.8	14.7	14.6	17.5	23.2	21.5
Physical Sciences	12.8	14.3	13.8	14.5	15.0	14.8	14.7	14.0	14.3	13.2	13.2
Engineering	11.9	13.4	11.8	11.7	12.6	11.9	12.6	11.4	11.8	10.7	11.
Social Sciences & History	4.0	4.2	4.6	4.6	4.3	3.9	3.6	4.5	4.1	3.3	4.0
Agriculture	3.4	3.5	4.1	4.0	3.4	3.6	3.9	3.4	3.9	3.1	3.7
Computer & Information Sciences	2.3	2.7	2.2	2.9	2.5	2.9	2.7	3.3	3.2	3.7	3.1
Other	3.1	1.5	1.6	2.2	1.5	3.3	2.8	2.4	1.9	2.2	2.7
Business & Management	2.8	2.9	2.6	2.5	2.3	2.4	2.5	3.1	2.9	3.8	2.7
Mathematics	2.5	2.8	2.8	2.9	2.8	2.6	2.5	2.6	2.7	2.4	2.4
Foreign Languages & Literature	2.3	2.0	2.3	1.9	2.3	2.8	1.9	2.0	2.5	1.9	1.9
Education	1.8	1.6	1.4	1.4	1.4	1.4	1.5	1.5	1.6	1.6	1.6
Area & Ethnic Studies	1.8	1.5	1.6	1.7	1.8	1.8	1.8	1.4	1.4	1.5	1.5
Psychology	0.9	0.9	0.8	1.0	1.0	1.1	1.0	1.0	1.0	1.2	1.2
Law & Legal Studies	1.1	1.0	1.0	1.0	1.1	1.1	1.2	1.0	1.0	0.9	1.2
Visual & Performing Arts	1.2	1.7	1.5	1.5	1.4	1.3	1.2	1.3	1.1	1.1	1.1
Letters	1.4	1.7	1.8	1.6	1.5	1.4	1.3	1.4	1.1	1.4	1.0
Public Affairs	0.6	0.8	0.7	0.5	0.5	0.5	0.6	0.6	0.5	1.2	0.8
Communications	0.6	0.6	0.4	0.5	0.5	0.5	0.5	0.6	0.6	0.7	0.7
Philosophy & Religion	1.1	0.7	0.9	0.7	0.7	0.7	0.6	0.9	0.6	0.8	0.7
Architecture & Environmental Design	0.7	0.8	0.7	0.6	0.8	0.8	0.7	0.8	0.7	0.7	0.6
Home Economics	0.4	0.4	0.5	0.6	0.6	0.3	0.4	0.5	0.5	0.4	0.6
Library Sciences	0.2	0.2	0.3	0.3	0.3	0.3	0.3	0.3	0.3	0.3	0.3
Marketing	0.1	0.1	0.1	0.1	0.1	0.1	0.1	0.1	0.1	0.1	0.1
Total	58,074	59,403	62,354	65,494	70,501	74,571	79,651	86,015	84,281	82,905	89,634

41 MAJOR FIELD OF SPECIALIZATION OF INTERNATIONAL SCHOLARS, 1994/95 – 2004/05

METHODOLOGY

IN THIS SECTION

TABLE	SOURCE	PAGE
Table 42	Place of Origin Codes by Place of Origin Within World Region	88
Table 43	Field of Study Category Codes	90
Table 44	Institutions Surveyed and Type of Response, Selected Years 1964/65 – 2004/05	93
Table 45	Institutions Reporting International Students and Type of Response, 2002/03 – 2004/05	93
Table 46	Institutions Reporting International Students by Individual Variables, 2004/05	94
Table 47	Response Rate to Individual Variables: International Scholar Survey, 1996/97 – 2004/05	94
Table 48	Response Rate to Individual Variables: Study Abroad Survey, 1994/95 – 2003/04	95
Table 49	Response Rate to Individual Variables: Intensive English Program Survey, 2004	95

ABOUT THE SURVEY

History of the Census

Since its founding in 1919, the Institute of International Education (IIE) has conducted an annual census of international students in the United States. For the first 30 years, IIE and the Committee on Friendly Relations Among Foreign Students carried out this effort jointly. IIE's first independent publication of the results of the annual census was *Education for One World*, containing data for the 1948/49 academic year. It was renamed the *Open Doors Report on International Educational Exchange* in 1954/55, and began receiving support from the Bureau of Educational and Cultural Affairs in USIA (now U.S. Department of State) in the early 1970s. *Open Doors* has long been regarded as a comprehensive source for basic trends in international students, international scholars, and international students in Intensive English Programs in the U.S., as well as U.S. students studying abroad.

Country Classification System

The classification of places of origin into regional groupings that is used throughout this report is based on the Department of State's definitions of world regions and states [Table 42].[1]

1 See *www.state.gov* for more information.

Code	Place
1000	AFRICA
1100	Eastern Africa
1115	Burundi
1120	Comoros
1105	Djibouti
1195	Eritrea
1125	Ethiopia
1130	Kenya
1135	Madagascar
1140	Malawi
1145	Mauritius
1150	Mozambique
1155	Reunion
1165	Rwanda
1170	Seychelles
1175	Somalia
1180	Tanzania
1185	Uganda
1190	Zambia
1160	Zimbabwe
1200	Central Africa
1210	Angola
1220	Cameroon
1230	Central African Republic
1240	Chad
1250	Congo
1260	Equatorial Guinea
1270	Gabon
1280	São Tomé & Príncipe
1290	Congo (Former Zaire)
1300	North Africa
1310	Algeria
1330	Egypt
1340	Libya
1350	Morocco
1370	Sudan
1380	Tunisia
1360	Western Sahara
1400	Southern Africa
1410	Botswana
1420	Lesotho
1430	Namibia
1440	South Africa
1450	Swaziland
1500	Western Africa
1510	Benin
1585	Burkina Faso
1505	Cape Verde
1535	Côte d'Ivoire
1515	Gambia
1520	Ghana
1525	Guinea
1530	Guinea-Bissau
1540	Liberia
1545	Mali
1550	Mauritania
1555	Niger
1560	Nigeria
1565	St. Helena
1570	Senegal
1575	Sierra Leone
1580	Togo
2000	ASIA
2100	East Asia
2110	China
2120	Taiwan
2130	Hong Kong
2140	Japan
2150	Korea, Democratic People's Republic of
2160	Korea, Republic of
2170	Macau
2180	Mongolia
2200	South & Central Asia
2205	Afghanistan
2210	Bangladesh
2215	Bhutan
2220	India
2260	Kazakhstan
2265	Kyrgyzstan
2225	Maldives
2230	Nepal
2235	Pakistan
2245	Sri Lanka
2270	Tajikistan
2250	Turkmenistan
2255	Uzbekistan
2300	Southeast Asia
2305	Brunei
2320	Cambodia
2315	Indonesia
2325	Laos
2330	Malaysia
2310	Myanmar
2335	Philippines
2345	Singapore
2350	Thailand

42 PLACE OF ORIGIN CODES BY PLACE OF ORIGIN WITHIN WORLD REGION

2360	Vietnam	3273	Portugal
2370	East Timor	3276	San Marino
		3280	Spain
3000	EUROPE	3283	Sweden
3100	Eastern Europe	3286	Switzerland
3110	Albania	3290	United Kingdom
3189	Armenia	3240	Vatican City
3174	Azerbaijan		
3181	Belarus	4000	LATIN AMERICA
3193	Bosnia & Herzegovina	4100	Caribbean
3120	Bulgaria	4103	Aruba
3191	Croatia	4105	Bahamas
3131	Czech Republic	4110	Barbados
3130	Czechoslovakia, Former*	4115	Cayman Islands
3183	Estonia	4120	Cuba
3188	Georgia	4125	Dominican Republic
3150	Hungary	4130	Guadeloupe
3184	Latvia	4135	Haiti
3185	Lithuania	4140	Jamaica
3194	Macedonia	4150	Leeward Islands
3187	Moldova	4155	Anguilla
3160	Poland	4151	Antigua
3170	Romania	4152	British Virgin Islands
3186	Russia	4153	Montserrat
3195	Serbia & Montenegro/Kosovo	4154	St. Kitts-Nevis
3132	Slovakia	4160	Martinique
3192	Slovenia	4170	Netherlands Antilles
3182	Ukraine	4180	Trinidad & Tobago
3180	U.S.S.R., Former*	4185	Turks & Caicos Isles
3190	Yugoslavia, Former*	4190	Windward Islands
3200	Western Europe	4191	Dominica
3203	Andorra	4192	Grenada
3206	Austria	4193	St. Lucia
3210	Belgium	4194	St. Vincent
3213	Denmark	4200	Central America & Mexico
3220	Finland	4210	Belize
3223	France	4230	Costa Rica
3226	Germany	4240	El Salvador
3233	Gibraltar	4250	Guatemala
3236	Greece	4260	Honduras
3243	Iceland	4270	Mexico
3246	Ireland	4280	Nicaragua
3250	Italy	4290	Panama
3253	Liechtenstein	4300	South America
3256	Luxembourg	4305	Argentina
3260	Malta	4310	Bolivia
3263	Monaco	4315	Brazil
3266	Netherlands	4320	Chile
3270	Norway	4325	Colombia

42 (cont'd) PLACE OF ORIGIN CODES BY PLACE OF ORIGIN WITHIN WORLD REGION

Fields of Study

The fields of study used in this book are from the *Classification of Instructional Programs, 2000*, published by the National Center for Education Statistics (NCES) of the U.S. Department of Education.[2] See Table 43 for a list of major fields of study.

Carnegie Classification System

Starting with *Open Doors 2004*, IIE began using the 2000 Carnegie Classifications, or codes.[3] Previously, IIE used the 1994 Carnegie codes. In the change from the 1994 to the 2000 editions of the codes, the Carnegie Classification system changed some institutions' codes, and some of the categories themselves were revised. Because *Open Doors* uses the Carnegie system for its rankings, as well as for various analyses, comparisons to some editions of *Open Doors* cannot readily be made.[4]

About the Annual Census of International Students

For the purposes of the Census, an international student is defined as an individual who is enrolled for courses at a higher education institution in the United States on a temporary visa, and who is not an immigrant (permanent resident with an I-151 or "Green Card"), a citizen, an illegal alien (undocumented immigrant), or a refugee.

2 For more information about the codes, see *www.nces.ed.gov/ pubs2002/cip2000*.

3 Carnegie Foundation for the Advancement of Teaching, *The Carnegie Classifications of Institutions of Higher Education, 2000 Edition*. Electronic Data File, Fourth Revision, 2003.

4 See *www.carnegiefoundation.org/classification* for a fuller discussion about the Carnegie Classification system.

For *Open Doors 2005*, IIE made three changes designed to improve data quality. First, the number of regionally accredited institutions surveyed was expanded, from 2,675 to 2,898, using data from the Integrated Postsecondary Education Data System (IPEDS) data, produced by the U.S. Department of Education *[http://nces.ed.gov/ipeds]*, with an additional check against the Department of Homeland Security's (DHS) SEVIS system *[http:// www.ice.gov/graphics/sevis/ index.htm]*. Second, the Census was made available in both electronic and hard-copy format. Third, the instructions were greatly expanded and clarified. Both were made available through the *Open Doors* website.

The Census was administered in Winter-Spring 2005 to 2,898 institutions. From the original 2,675 institutions, we obtained a response rate of 73.0%; from the 223 new institutions, the response rate was 39.9%. Overall, 2,042 or 70.5% responded to the survey [Table 44]. Anecdotal reports from institutions revealed that the expansion of SEVIS data collection, among other reasons, might have affected response rates. However, the response rates, which are the product of five mail follow-ups, in addition to extensive e-mail and telephone follow-ups (four rounds each), are very high for electronic, web-based surveys.

Almost 96% (1,958) of the responding institutions reported enrolling international students [Table 44]. Of these institutions, 15% (298) provided only total international student counts (Step

4330	Ecuador
4335	Falkland Islands
4340	French Guiana
4345	Guyana
4350	Paraguay
4355	Peru
4360	Suriname
4365	Uruguay
4370	Venezuela
2400	**MIDDLE EAST**
2405	Bahrain
2410	Cyprus
2415	Iran
2420	Iraq
2425	Israel
2430	Jordan
2435	Kuwait
2440	Lebanon
2445	Oman
2443	Palestinian Authority
2450	Qatar
2455	Saudi Arabia
2460	Syria
2465	Turkey
2470	United Arab Emirates
2485	Yemen
5000	**NORTH AMERICA**
5110	Bermuda
5120	Canada

6000	**OCEANIA**
6100	Australia/New Zealand
6110	Australia
6120	New Zealand
6200	**Pacific Ocean Island Are**
6210	Cook Islands
6215	Fiji
6220	French Polynesia
6225	Kiribati
6227	Marshall Islands
6260	Micronesia, Federated States of
6230	Nauru
6235	New Caledonia
6250	Niue
6255	Norfolk Island
6263	Palau
6240	Papua New Guinea
6205	Solomon Islands
6270	Tonga
6271	Tuvalu
6245	Vanuatu
6275	Wallis & Futuna Isles
6280	Western Samoa
7000	**ANTARCTICA**
9999	**UNKNOWN**

Note: Code for "Canary Islands" deleted New Code for "Serbia & Montenegro/Kosovo" added
*Some students are still reported under former country classificatio

42 **(cont'd) PLACE OF ORIGIN CODES BY PLACE OF ORIGIN WITHIN WORLD REGION**

AGRICULTURE
01   Agriculture, Agriculture Operations, and Related Sciences
03   Conservation and Renewable Natural Resources

ARCHITECTURE AND RELATED PROGRAMS
04   Architecture and Related Services

AREA, ETHNIC, CULTURAL, AND GENDER STUDIES
05   Area, Ethnic, Cultural, and Gender Studies

BUSINESS MANAGEMENT AND ADMINISTRATIVE SERVICES
52   Business, Management, Marketing, and Related Support Services

COMMUNICATIONS
09   Communications, Journalism, and Related Programs

43 **FIELD OF STUDY CATEGORY CODES**

10   Communication Technologies/Technicians and Support Services

COMPUTER AND INFORMATION SCIENCES
11   Computer and Information Sciences and Support Services

PERSONAL AND CULINARY SERVICES
12   Personal and Culinary Services

EDUCATION
13   Education

ENGINEERING
14   Engineering
15   Engineering Technologies/Technicians

FOREIGN LANGUAGES AND LITERATURE
16   Foreign Languages, Literature, and Linguistics

HEALTH
51   Health Professions and Related Clinical Services

HOME ECONOMICS
19   Family and Consumer Sciences/Human Sciences

LAW AND LEGAL STUDIES
22   Legal Profession and Studies

ENGLISH LANGUAGE AND LITERATURE/LETTERS
23   English Language and Literature/Letters

LIBERAL/GENERAL STUDIES
24   Liberal Arts and Sciences, General Studies, and Humanities

LIBRARY SCIENCES
25   Library Sciences

LIFE SCIENCES
26   Biological and Biomedical Sciences

MATHEMATICS
27   Mathematics and Statistics

MILITARY TECHNOLOGIES
28   R.O.T.C. (Reserve Officer Training Corps)
29   Military Technologies

MULTI/INTERDISCIPLINARY STUDIES
30   Multi/Interdisciplinary Studies

PARKS, RECREATION, LEISURE, AND FITNESS STUDIES
31   Parks, Recreation, and Fitness Studies

PHILOSOPHY AND RELIGIOUS STUDIES
38   Philosophy
39   Theological Studies and Religious Vocations

PHYSICAL SCIENCES
40   Physical Sciences
41   Science Technologies/Technicians

43   (cont'd) FIELD OF STUDY CATEGORY CODES

1) [Table 45]. The majority (85%), however, provided information not only on the total but also on the students' place of origin, field of study, academic level, sex, and other characteristics (Step 2). The Step 2 response rate is the second highest in three years. The vast majority of the institutions with international students sent data on some or all of the characteristics on the questionnaire [Table 46]. Data on academic level and place of origin exist for almost 100%. On other key variables – visa status, sex, field of study, and enrollment – the response rate was over 90%. Conversely, the rate for students' primary source of funding was 51%, and that for marital status only 41%.

About the International Scholar Survey

For the purposes of this survey, international scholars are defined as non-immigrant, non-student academics (teachers and/or researchers, administrators) in the U.S. Scholars may be affiliated with U.S. institutions for other activities such as conferences, colloquia, observations, consultations, or other short-term professional development activities, but the survey was limited to doctoral degree-granting institutions where most J Visa scholars were based. This online survey captured data for the period beginning on July 1, 2004 and ending June 30, 2005. Institutions were asked about the primary function of the scholars (research, teaching, both, or other), geographic origin, field of specialization, sex, and visa status.

Responses were received from 198 of the 354 institutions polled, for a response rate of 56%. Based on the past practice of estimating for non-response for this survey [see below, "Imputation and Estimation"], data from 43 additional institutions (overall totals only) were included, and thus 68% of the institutions were represented in the analysis. Most institutions reporting international scholars in 2004/05 were able to provide detailed information on the characteristics of their scholars, and the response rates for the various survey items far exceeded those seen in years past [Table 47]. The proportion of institutions that provided breakdowns for individual variables ranged from almost 100% for visa status to over 79% for primary function.

About the U.S. Study Abroad Survey

The study abroad population is defined as only those students (U.S. citizens and permanent residents) enrolled for a degree at a U.S. accredited higher education institution, who received academic credit for study abroad from their home institution upon their return. Students studying abroad without credit are not included here, nor are U.S. students enrolled overseas for degrees. Hence, the figures presented here give a conservative picture of study abroad activity.

The changes that were made to the International Student Census, discussed above, were also made for the U.S. Study Abroad Survey (with the exception of cross checks against SEVIS). The number

PSYCHOLOGY
42   Psychology

SECURITY AND PROTECTIVE SERVICES
43   Protective Services

PUBLIC ADMINISTRATION AND SOCIAL SERVICE PROFESSIONS
44   Public Administration and Services

SOCIAL SCIENCES AND HISTORY
45   Social Sciences
54   History

TRADE AND INDUSTRIAL
46   Construction Trades
47   Mechanics and Repairs
48   Precision Production
49   Transportation and Material Moving

VISUAL AND PERFORMING ARTS
50   Visual and Performing Arts

RESIDENCY PROGRAMS
60   Residency Programs

UNDECLARED
90   Undeclared

OPTIONAL PRACTICAL TRAINING
95*   Optional Practical Training

INTENSIVE ENGLISH
99**   Intensive English

Source: National Center for Education Statistics, *Classification of Instructional Programs, 2000* (Washington, D.C.: NCES, 2001). Web address: *www.nces.ed.gov/pubs2002/cip2000*.

* Code created to capture Optional Practical Training (OPT), which is not represented among the CIP 2000 codes.

** Code created to capture Intensive English, which is not represented among the CIP 2000 codes.

43   (cont'd) FIELD OF STUDY CATEGORY CODES

of institutions surveyed was increased from 1,308 to 1,465 institutions. Study abroad data was obtained from 887 or 61% of the 1,465 surveyed institutions for the 2003/04 academic year, including summer 2004. Of the 887, 858 (66%) came from the original 1,308 institutions and the remaining 29 (19%) came from the additional 157 new institutions.

While lower than last year's rate of 78%, it nonetheless represents a substantial response resulting from repeated requests for data. This included five mail follow-ups, two rounds each of phone and e-mail follow-ups, as well as assistance from the NAFSA Education Abroad Data Collection Committee.

Year	Institutions Surveyed	Institutions w/ Int'l Students	Institutions w/o Int'l Students	Total Responding Institutions	% Response
1964/65	2,556	1,859	434	2,293	89.7
1969/70	2,859	1,734	265	1,999	69.9
1974/75	3,085	1,760	148	1,908	61.8
1979/80	3,186	2,651	299	2,950	92.6
1984/85	2,833	2,492	274	2,766	97.6
1989/90	2,891	2,546	294	2,840	98.2
1990/91	2,879	2,543	241	2,784	96.7
1991/92	2,823	2,436	228	2,646	94.4
1992/93	2,783	2,417	166	2,583	92.8
1993/94	2,743	2,451	163	2,614	95.3
1994/95	2,758	2,517	167	2,684	97.3
1995/96	2,715	2,403	176	2,579	95.7
1996/97	2,732	2,428	185	2,613	95.6
1997/98	2,726	2,394	177	2,571	94.3
1998/99	2,708	2,446	142	2,588	95.6
1999/00	2,696	2,367	126	2,493	92.5
2000/01	2,699	2,344	120	2,464	91.3
2001/02	2,697	2,284	100	2,384	88.4
2002/03	2,697	2,307	113	2,420	90.0
2003/04	2,685	2,225	118	2,345	87.3
2004/05	2,898	1,958	84	2,042	70.5

44 INSTITUTIONS SURVEYED AND TYPE OF RESPONSE, SELECTED YEARS 1964/65 – 2004/05

Type of Response	2002/03 Total	2002/03 %	2003/04 Total	2003/04 %	2004/05 Total	2004/05 %
Total Only – STEP 1	445	17.7	281	12.6	298	14.6
Institutional Data – STEP 2	1,862	82.3	1,944	87.4	1,744	85.4
Total with Students	**2,307**		**2,225**		**2,042**	

45 INSTITUTIONS REPORTING INTERNATIONAL STUDENTS AND TYPE OF RESPONSE, 2002/03 – 2004/05

data to capture undergraduate completions. After the IPEDS and study abroad survey files are matched, participation is calculated by dividing the total number of undergraduates in study abroad in a given year by the total number of undergraduate completions.[5] This is a proxy estimate of the proportion of students in a two- or four-year cohort that goes through a study abroad experience at least once during their academic career.

About the Intensive English Program Survey

IIE and two leading professional Intensive English Program (IEP) associations, the American Association of Intensive English Programs (AAIEP) and the University and College Intensive English Programs (UCIEP), collaborated to collect national data that reflect IEP activity in the U.S. Data elements in this survey include program sponsorship, the percentage of students intending to continue further (non-IEP) study in the U.S., program duration (18 hours or more, 18 hours or fewer), and place of origin. Student totals reflect both headcount enrollment and enrollment by "student-weeks." One student-week equals one student studying for one week.

Non-AAIEP and UCIEP institutions were also invited to participate in the survey. These IEPs were taken from IIE's

Most of the institutions provided detailed information about the characteristics of the students [Table 48]. The proportion of institutions that gave breakdowns for individual variables ranged from slightly under 55% for race/ethnicity to almost 97% for duration of study. For the first time, the survey included questions designed to capture study abroad activity in the current academic year (2004/05). Of the institutions reporting any study abroad activity, 87% were able to provide 2004/05 data. Of that 87%, 63% estimated their totals while the remaining 37% were able to provide actual figures.

Participation rates: The undergraduate participation calculations use IPEDS

5 For *Open Doors 2005*, the IPEDS completion data were consistent with the U.S. Study Abroad Survey reporting academic year: that is, both reflected activity in 2003/04.

Intensive English USA (IEUSA) 2005 directory. In all, 680 programs were contacted by e-mail and and returns were obtained from 194 programs for an overall response rate of 29%, a decline over last year's rate of 37%. The 44,565 students reported this year reflect student enrollments throughout the 2004 calendar year (January 1, 2004 to December 31, 2004). The mix of reporting institutions reflects university and college-affiliated programs as well as large for-profit entities that offer English language training. As with our other surveys, not all programs providing total numbers could provide detailed breakouts of duration of study by number of students (79% of students), duration of study in student-weeks (79% of programs), and the percent of students pursuing further study (72% of programs) [Table 49].

Category	Base Number	% of Int'l Students
Academic Level	564,062	99.8
Field of Study	526,500	93.2
Sex	523,204	92.6
Place of Origin	562,843	99.6
Enrollment Status	518,940	91.8
Visa Status	528,818	93.6
Primary Source of Funds	289,133	51.2
Marital Status	232,897	41.2
Total Reported	**565,039**	

46 INSTITUTIONS REPORTING INTERNATIONAL STUDENTS BY INDIVIDUAL VARIABLES, 2004/05

	1996/97 %	1997/98 %	1998/99 %	1999/00 %	2000/01 %	2001/02 %	2002/03 %	2003/04 %	2004/05 %
Visa Status	92.9	84.2	94.8	70.4	85.5	76.7	66.1	89.6	98.8
Place of Origin	90.8	83.6	88.9	94.5	82.3	71.7	63.6	77.4	90.9
Sex	88.3	80.2	82.9	64.8	79.4	70.8	58.0	89.6	87.8
Primary Function	88.2	69.2	81.9	67.7	76.9	70.3	57.4	78.3	79.2
Field of Specialization	88.4	84.0	87.8	65.9	78.9	67.3	56.1	68.8	81.9
Total Reported	**62,354**	**65,494**	**70,501**	**74,571**	**79,651**	**86,015**	**84,281**	**82,905**	**89,634**

47 RESPONSE RATE TO INDIVIDUAL VARIABLES: INTERNATIONAL SCHOLAR SURVEY, 1996/97 – 2004/05

Imputation and Estimation

Throughout this publication, total international student enrollments, U.S. study abroad totals, international scholar totals, IEP totals, and the various percentages herein are calculated directly from campus-based survey responses. Other student counts are determined by imputation, since not all campuses are able to provide detailed breakdowns by the various categories, such as place of origin, field of study, etc. Estimates of the number of students for each of the variables collected by the various surveys are imputed from the total number of students reported. For each imputation, base or raw counts are multiplied by a correction factor that reflects the ratio of difference between the sum of the categories being imputed and the total number of students reported by institutions. For this reason, student totals may vary slightly within this publication. In addition, due to rounding, percentages do not always add up to 100% (whether or not numbers are imputed).

The data collection methodology was designed to produce stable, national estimates of international education activity. Analysis for units that reflect relatively small numbers of students (certain places of origin, fields of study, sources of financial support) and especially those that are cut by other variables may reflect greater error variation than variables with a larger response base. In addition, to account for potential instability in annual institution-level counts, estimates based on counts

Category	1994/95 %	1995/96 %	1996/97 %	1997/98 %	1998/99 %	1999/00 %	2000/01 %	2001/02 %	2002/03 %	2003/04 %
Duration of Study	77.7	91.2	89.8	85.9	89.5	92.5	92.1	93.0	69.9	96.5
Host Destination	79.5	91.0	88.4	80.6	86.3	92.2	91.4	91.0	86.3	95.4
Program Sponsorship	73.8	92.2	88.7	86.2	87.2	91.0	89.6	90.0	67.4	93.5
Academic Level	63.6	77.8	78.5	78.1	79.2	82.5	83.1	80.2	62.2	95.7
Sex	65.6	76.1	75.1	75.9	76.3	81.0	80.3	80.2	78.2	85.2
Field of Study	45.9	60.2	62.8	65.1	65.6	75.1	80.5	77.6	55.3	84.8
Race/Ethnicity	33.0	39.7	40.9	42.6	44.8	45.7	50.3	47.7	57.2	54.8
Total Reported	**84,403**	**89,242**	**99,448**	**113,959**	**129,770**	**143,590**	**154,168**	**160,920**	**174,629**	**191,321**

48 RESPONSE RATE TO INDIVIDUAL VARIABLES: STUDY ABROAD SURVEY, 1994/95 – 2003/04

Category	# of Reporting Programs	% of All Participating Programs
Program Type	194	100.0
Total Number of Students	194	100.0
Total number of Student-Weeks	194	100.0
Number of Students by Place of Origin	194	100.0
Number of Student-Weeks by Place of Origin	194	100.0
Duration of Study, Number of Students	143	79.0
Duration of Study, Number of Student-Weeks	143	79.0
Percent of Students Pursuing Further Study	130	71.8

49 RESPONSE RATE TO INDIVIDUAL VARIABLES: INTENSIVE ENGLISH PROGRAM SURVEY, 2004

from the previous reporting year (if available) are sometimes used to account for any given non-reporting institution, but only if there is a history of reporting to *Open Doors* surveys and the previous year's figures were not estimated. For International Students and Study Abroad, these estimates are based upon the prior year's number adjusted by the average percent change among institutions that reported in the prior and current academic years. For International Scholars counts, esti-

mates to account for non-reporting campuses were based on numbers reported in the previous year (if available and not estimated itself), with no additional adjustment. The only case where estimation was not performed was for Intensive English: unlike the other survey data presented in this current volume, and consistent with last year's practices, no estimates were produced to account for IEP non-reporting. While estimation refinements were made for this edition and will continue

to be made for future editions, the general practice of estimating based on previous years' numbers is entirely consistent with past years' *Open Doors* analysis protocols.

Differences exist between the sum of undergraduate/graduate breakdowns by place of origin [Table 2] and the "official" aggregate undergraduate/graduate totals [Table 18]. The official figure is based on data from each reporting U.S. institution of their total enrollment of international students by academic level. While most institutions report academic level breakdowns by place of origin, others are unable to do so. The data shown in Table 2 are adjusted only to the extent to which institutions are able to provide academic level data by place of origin. In practice, *Open Doors* does not adjust further for this discrepancy, and uses the overall academic level, not the academic level by place of origin, as the basis for calculating changes from year to year and for analyses.

ACKNOWLEDGMENTS

Producing the *Open Doors Report* involves the cooperation and contributions of many individuals and organizations. The Bureau of Educational and Cultural Affairs of the U.S. Department of State has provided funding for the project since the 1970s. This grant enables the Institute to collect, analyze, publish, and disseminate the data on international students, U.S. students abroad, and international scholars in the *Open Doors* publication and online. The American Association of Intensive English Programs (AAIEP) and University and College Intensive English Programs (UCIEP), two leading intensive English language program organizations, have provided support to the Institute to collect and report data on international students in Intensive English Programs since 1999.

The American Association of Collegiate Registrars and Admissions Officers, College Board, Council of Graduate Schools, and NAFSA: Association of International Educators, serve on the advisory committee for *Open Doors*. Glenn Cerosaletti, Chair, and the rest of NAFSA's Education Abroad Data Collection Committee worked with the Institute to continue to improve reporting among study abroad data providers. Alan Turner, Vice-President for Advocacy at AAIEP and Richard Schreck, Advocacy at UCIEP, assisted in publicizing the IEP Survey to their members and in encouraging responses to the survey. Jason Baumgartner and Lynn Schoch of Indiana University at Bloomington analyzed the economic impact of international students in the U.S. Without the work of thousands of colleagues at institutions across the U.S. who provide the data, *Open Doors* would not be the comprehensive and reliable data source that it has been for decades.

Several individuals outside of the Institute assisted in the production process. Patricia Chow and Robin Koo worked to ensure that the data was as accurate as possible. Lenora Komlacevs at DRS Imaging oversaw the data entry. Renée Meyer, of Renée Meyer Graphics, designed the finished product. Lori Gilbert and Alan Flint at Automated Graphic Systems assisted with the printing process.

At the Institute, Peggy Blumenthal, Executive Vice-President, provides overall guidance for the project. Sharon Witherell, assisted by Hannah Thompson at the Institute and Deborah Gardner at Halstead Communications, are instrumental in disseminating the report to a wider audience beyond the field of international education. Daniel Obst, assisted by Toby Rugger, maintains the *Open Doors* site on IIENetwork.org and prepared some of the global competition data. Dr. Adria Gallup-Black, the outgoing Director of Research & Evaluation, analyzed the data. Dr. Rajika Bhandari, the incoming director, reviewed the text.

We at the Institute hope that *Open Doors* continues to serve as a useful information resource to those within the field of international education, as well as to others outside the field who have an interest in international educational exchanges.

Hey-Kyung Koh Chin
Editor, *Open Doors*
Senior Program Officer, Research & Evaluation
Institute of International Education

New York City
December 2005